These Wonderful People of Xinjiang

Lisa Carducci

Foreign Languages Press

First Edition   2008

Except where mentionned, all photos were provided by Lisa Carducci.

ISBN 978-7-119-05180-2

Foreign Languages Press, Beijing, China
Published by Foreign Languages Press
24 Baiwanzhuang Road, Beijing 100037, China
Home Page:
http://www.flp.com.cn
E-mail Addresses:
info@flp.com.cn
sales@flp.com.cn

Distributed by China International Book Trading Corporation
35 Chegongzhuang Xilu, Beijing 100044, China
P.O. Box 399, Beijing, China

Printed in the People's Republic of China

TABLE OF CONTENTS

Introduction ✳

It was 1993, the first time. I was accompanying one of my students of Italian to her hometown, Urumqi, for the summer holidays. We reached our destination after 72 hours on the train. In the passing years, rail transportation has improved to the point where one can make the distance in 60 hours, and 48 hours, presently. Living conditions have also improved and more people travel by plane now.

The second time, it was 2005; then, I spent 11 days in Xinjiang. Today, July 4, 2007, I leave Beijing to realize a long-harbored dream: to live in Xinjiang for more than one month. In three and a half hours, I fly the 2,842 km between the two airports.

The sky is blue... a glowing and indefinable blue. We fly over a layer of clouds that look like a flock of sheep. And immediately I see myself among the sheep breeders on the summer pasture. And when I see another kind of cloud formation, like cotton balls, I am transported to the eternal snows of the 18,600 glaciers, big and small, of the Xinjiang Uyghur Autonomous Region. Elsewhere, a flat sheet of immaculate white is pierced by peaks of "whipped cream," which remind me of yurts (tent houses).

Suddenly, between the clouds, I see spots of ochre: the desert. They become larger and larger. There are no longer any clouds, only sand. The desert... sometimes as flat as a beach, sometimes striated with scars left by the wind or with the 600 km of roads that once served mainly for oil transportation, or sometimes covered with dunes as in images from my childhood. Yesterday, the *China Daily* newspaper reported on the increasingly serious desertification in Xinjiang – 1.03 million sq km in this region suffer greatly from land erosion. Desertification affects 80 out of the 90 counties and cities and almost two-thirds of the territory. At least 12 million persons suffer the consequences – from the lack of drinkable water to the soil aridity. Sand occupies one-third of the reservoirs' capacity, and at least one-third of the arable land has become salt marsh. The desert area expands by 100 sq km a year. Also, to avoid the silting of the roads, herbs have been planted in square plots to dam the sand and, in some places, the herbs have succeeded in "greening" the area. This is visible from high in the air, in the middle of nowhere. In the last six years, 2.3 billion sq m of water have been diverted to save the threatened vegetation along the Tarim River. Xinjiang has controlled erosion on more than 5,700 sq km of land. There is hope then.

It is in this region covering one-sixth of China's territory where 55 of the 56 nationalities, who compose the Chinese nation (all of them except the Jino), now live, where I have come to meet "ordinary" people, and find what is extraordinary in them – these wonderful Xinjiang people.

(Boarding flight CUA-2273)

THE LOVER OF THE CELESTIAL MOUNTAINS

Tusipbek, Kazak

After the Uyghurs (more than 8 million), the Kazaks are the ethnic group that ranks second in number in Xinjiang with 1.25 million nationals.

Tall, with an erect bearing, thick hair, and even, very white teeth, Tusipbek (pronounced Tuʳs'bⁱek) welcomed me punctually at the entrance of his apartment with a wide smile. The 60-year-old man had just retired, but he did not spend his days in idleness, as we will see. Tusipbek was not the type of man who sought publicity; he displayed great modesty, even though he had been interviewed several times in the past few years. As he was not very talkative, I had to extract his revelations one by one.

His wife, who is rather small, with brilliant eyes that captured my attention, is called Hanipa. I asked them about their family name, and I learned that Kazaks of both sexes just add their father's given name after their own, but it is not necessary to mention it except in official situations. For example, their son's name is Ayden·Tuspbek. Here I must clarify something for the rest of the book. Written Kazak language uses the Arabic alphabet in Xinjiang, while in Kazakhstan, people use the Slavic characters. When it comes to a phonetic translation in the Western alphabet, the Xinjiang Kazak use Latin alphabet mixed with Cyrillic. When Ayden had his name cards printed for international use, he chose to write his father's name without an "i," in such a way to make it easy to read and memorize for the people of different countries and languages he has contact with. In the present gallery of portraits, I transcribed the names as I heard them, to be read using the English pronunciation.

Conversation took a while to really begin. At first, my two interlocutors answered with a "yes" or a "no" only. Did they fear the foreigner that I am? Were they timid by nature? I learned that their daughter Aixia married a doctor last year, also Kazak, whose name is Erken. The young couple live in an apartment they bought not far from their parents. Tusipbek and Hanipa also own their very comfortable and pleasant apartment. I envied the three carpets of different styles that cover

the living room, the dining room, and the hallway, which are all open space. The house was remarkably clean, and visitors, as well as the owners of the place, remove their shoes when they arrive.

Tusipbek is from Urumqi, while Hanipa, both Kazak and Muslim, was born in Altay, the administrative centre of the Altay Prefecture. She has lived in Urumqi for 30 years. When they were primary and middle school students, only the Kazak language was taught. It was when they entered university that they started learning Chinese as the national language. They could speak it a little but completely ignored the written language.

Tusipbek attended Minzu Daxue or University of Ethnic Minorities in Beijing from 1962 to 1968. Then, for two years – in the middle of the "cultural revolution" – he was sent to the countryside to be "re-educated" by the peasants. Things went differently for Hanipa, who was born on the "right side," while Tusipbek came from a family with "bad origins," meaning that his father and mother were part of the *heiwulei*, or peoples' enemy, such as landowners, wealthy peasants, counter-revolutionaries, criminals, and rightists.

When I asked Tusipbek about the impressions he kept from these two years of re-education, he answered enthusiastically, "Oh! I learned lots of things! First, how to cook. We were three students living together and we had to manage. In another field, I was studying politics before; in the countryside, for sure, it was out of the question. I decided to become useful and I served as an

interpreter for the Kazak peasants who didn't know a word of Chinese. That gave me the idea, then, to compile a dictionary of botany and zoology for them, first a little one, and later this one, in Chinese and Latin to Kazak, written in Latin-Slavic phonetic alphabet. It adds up to over 800 pages."

Hanipa graduated from Xinjiang University in 1968. It was later that Tusipbek met her in the *chuanlian* (literally "establishing ties" or "making contacts") period, at the beginning of the "cultural revolution," when the Red Guards used to travel all around the country – and for free – to gather their forces and chase heads to cut off.

Their son, single then, still lives with them. He is a specialist in the Russian language. After several years with the regional information bureau, he had recently established a company of international commerce. Business was just starting and the staff numbered only a handful, but progress could be seen already. Surprised that Ayden had abandoned his Russian schooling for the business world, I asked the obvious question. Tusipbek clarified, "Ayden does business with Kazakhstan, Kirghizstan, Russia, where everyone works in Russian." The elder daughter, Aixia, is an employee in the financial field.

From 1971 to 1991, Tusipbek was an editor for the Kazak language section of the Renmin Chubanshe (People's Publishing House) where Hanipa also worked until her retirement. Then, he was with the *Xinjiang Ribao* (*Xinjiang Daily*) until 2006 when he retired. He used to be deputy editor-in-chief with the title of senior reporter. But Tusipbek had remained active, as I could tell when he pointed to a pile of 100 envelopes that were ready to be mailed and that contained negatives or photos for the illustrated section of his former journal. His cooperation is deeply appreciated and he offers it willingly, because photography is much more than a hobby for him. It is a passion!

Under my eyes Tusipbek turned the pages of what seemed to be his favourite work, *An Overview of Kazak Folk Customs*, which required a decade of preparation. This large book speaks with images of landscapes, cultural relics, ballad singers, traditional clothing and accessories, literature and art, yurts (or "felt houses") as family homes, musical instruments, handicrafts, games and sports, tourism, hunters, fauna and flora, sciences and technologies, culture, education, health, agriculture and husbandry, developing market, food and, finally, Nature's masterpieces. It is not without basis that Tusipbek is known as a photographer: he is the producer of 20,000 photos about the Kazak people.

Yet, it was only for recreation that Tusipbek started taking photos when he was a university student. Up to now, more than 5,000 of his photos have been published,

six of them winning an international prize and 40, a national prize. In May 2007, Tusipbek was invited to the Great Hall of the People in Beijing during an exhibition on Xinjiang in the national capital and the presentation of an album on Kanas – a wonderful natural region in the north of Xinjiang – to which he had generously contributed.

Also, in 1993, he wrote in the Kazak language a handbook of tricks and tips for photo enthusiasts, and another modest work in 2003 on hard-to-access places that he had visited. When Tusipbek leaves for a photo expedition, he leaves for 10, 30, or 60 days. With one or two companions, and with as little luggage as possible, a horse drawing a sled, and a dog, this explorer moves forward with difficulty through the thick layer of soft snow, with his equipment on his back, climbs slopes that the horse can't traverse, and changes the films with his bare hands at temperatures of -30 or -40°C, because wearing gloves restricts freedom of movement. Where he goes, there is neither a hotel nor an inn. Sometimes he walks the whole night long with only melted snow to drink. Sometimes the explorer stops behind the sled, illuminated by the moon, and eats a piece of *nang* (bread) with *sarmai* (butter). Sometimes he finds an opportunity in a village where he can enjoy a herdsman's hospitality. In that case, he can let the horse rest for one or two days and buy hay for the rest of the voyage.

A mountain lover, Tusipbek spent three years exploring the Altay Mountains in the north, two years in the mountain ranges of Kunlun in the south, and seven years in the Tianshan Mountains in the centre of Xinjiang – all to dislodge their secrets and to embed them on film.

He considers himself first as the explorer of the Tianshan Mountains, and it is he himself who suggested to me the title of this chapter. Tianshan means "Celestial Mountains," in fact. It was easy to feel his burning passion for the high mountains and his deep love for the incomparable ranges of Tianshan in particular.

When we see the photographs taken by Tusipbek, we can understand that with so much beauty around him in his own region, the photographer doesn't feel the need to

go elsewhere. However, he was invited for one week in Kazakhstan in 2003 for an exhibition, and he also went for trips related to his work to Malaysia, Singapore, and Thailand. He participates in special festivals such as the great cultural event that takes place every four years and that will reunite all the Kazak people and their horses in Qoqek (Tacheng) on August 8. As I would not be able to attend the great rallying, Tusipbek handed over a copy of his book on the Kazak people, "Here, this is for you."

What makes Tusipbek, as he stated it himself, a particular man and especially a favoured photographer, is that he was born in the countryside and he spent his childhood in the mountains. He has mastered four

languages (Kazak, Chinese, Uyghur, and Mongolian) and has no problems with communication. Finally, he grew up "on horseback" as is characteristic of these people and dismisses transportation problems. "Moreover", he said laughingly, "20 kilometres a day, even with luggage, have never been an obstacle."

In 1994, the photographer was followed for 10 days by CCTV-10 while his camera hunted polar bears and black bears. The bear represents a danger to man when it has a cub, when it is eating, and when it is in the mating season. One must carry a hunting knife and a rifle to be prepared for all such contingencies.

Tusipbek faced all kinds of dangers: in addition to the bears are rain and lightning, which means absolutely halting photography and the crossing of creeks or streams. Once, his horse slipped and was wounded, bleeding from the muzzle. Tusipbek had to continue on foot, with rain-drenched material and equipment. The wolves, which fear man, do not pose a threat. Another challenge is to wait patiently, several hours sometimes, without moving, without eating, for favourable light – the *exact* light – to start the objective of the camera.

I asked Tusipbek whether he liked anything other than photography. He answered that he liked to dance: folklore and especially modern dance. He was not short of projects and was thinking about producing another

important work titled "Marvellous Xinjiang," a book on special places that very few know, with directions on how to go there.

More than an hour passed since Hanipa had disappeared from the room; then, from the kitchen seeped a fragrant aroma of boiled lamb. Suddenly she came out with a joyous "*cha'is*" (To the tea!). Contrary to my Italian, Canadian, and even Chinese practices, the meal began with a variety of cream pastries, honey or goat butter biscuits, rolls filled with wild grape or raspberry jam – this berry unknown in China except in Xinjiang. The milk tea was not that of the Tibetans or of the Mongols, but red tea (black) with fresh milk, without salt or sugar. After these cocktail snacks came the "real" dishes, meaning rice with carrots and turnips and lamb that one eats with the hands (*zhua fan*). We ended with *kurt* (cheese),

Photo : Tusipbek

susbei (drained yogurt, almost dry) which functions to cut through the grease, and the sweetest melon I had ever tasted: the *tiangua*, which bears its name perfectly.

Hanipa happily explained to me that the butter is made in a leather churn, a flexible quadrangle, and is preserved frozen, wrapped in a thin goatskin.

When I left Tusipbek's and Hanipa's home, my vocabulary had increased with a few Kazak words: *A ke*, *A pa*, *A pai*, respectively Dad, Mom, and Aunt, and my weight had increased, too – by several grams certainly.

COOKING, NOTHING ELSE

Tursun·Mammet Hadji, Uyghur

Born in Hotan ("Hetian" in Chinese) on March 17, 1951, Tursun claimed he was influenced by his father at a young age. His father, a Hadji, meaning that he has accomplished the pilgrimage, *hadj*, to Mecca, owned a restaurant, and Tursun, the eldest of 12 children, started to cook at the age of 12. His mother, with eight daughters and four sons, certainly had no time to work outside the home, not even to help her husband in the restaurant.

Tursun attended primary and middle school, in the Uyghur language exclusively. He learned Chinese from his colleagues when he started to work. Today, he speaks it with a strong accent and can read some but not write it. This detail may interest especially the readers who still believe in the Sinitic standardization of all the ethnic groups of the country.

All of Tursun's brothers and sisters still live in Hotan – home of white jade and roses. He is the only one who lives in Urumqi.

At 20, Tursun was called up for military service and remained there from 1972 to 1977. During his service, he cooked for his comrades and worked as a chef for two years with the Bianjiang Hotel under the army.

In the national capital, each province and autonomous region of the country has a guesthouse where their citizens stay when they go to Beijing for business. Tursun worked with the Xinjiang Banshichu (Hotel), in Beijing, for two years. In 1980, he returned to Xinjiang where he continued to be a cook for the Urumqi Manpower Centre until 1985.

Then 34 years old, he opened his own restaurant and bought an apartment that he kept until 2004. He finally sold it because it was too large, and he bought a smaller one – 160 sq m – with three bedrooms.

It did not take a century for Tursun to become very prosperous. However, he remains modest, doesn't criticize his competitors, and doesn't pride himself on his achievements. In 20 years, five other restaurants were added to the main establishment: King of the *zhua fan*, 17 Wu Yi (May 1st) Avenue – in Urumqi, Shihezi, Bole, Changji, and Shawan. Tursun trusts the managers of his

branches, whom he contacts by Internet without having to go the locations physically. His son, who specialized in financial administration, has been working with him since he graduated, while his daughter, a tradesman's wife, is unemployed. She did not pass the university admission exam. Her father wanted her to continue her studies, as he thinks it is as important for a girl as for a boy to be highly educated. However, he found neither shame nor despair in this failure: Chinese students are legion, while university admissions are limited.

At the main restaurant, 20 employees, all Uyghurs, serve 200-300 customers a day, a large majority being Han. Tursun doesn't serve alcohol or allow smoking, but he tolerates beer in reasonable amounts for the non-Muslims. The Chinese and foreign tourists are numerous and they make reservations long before they arrive. The customers flow between 13:00 and 15:00 and the evening, from 19:00 to closing at 10:00.

Of what does a man like Tursun dream? He is having built what is called in China "Dujiacun" or family vacation village; one in Urumqi and one in Korla ("Kuerle" in Chinese). They will be ready in two or three years. Meanwhile, trees will have time to grow, "because a *Dujiacun* without greenery is not worthy of this name," clarified the future hotel owner. "But you are a real businessman!" I said, to which Tursun retorted,

"Cooking, this is all that I can do!" He wants his establishments to be of a Muslim type, meaning without alcohol, tobacco, thundering music and people laughing and speaking loudly enough to burst the eardrums. For him, the most important priority in life is calm, peace. Of course, Muslim or not, all customers are welcome if they abide by the rules.

Tursun also owns a wool factory in the United Arab Emirates. He often goes there for business, as well as in

Iran, Turkey, Oman, and Pakistan. As he speaks only Uyghur and imperfect Chinese, he takes along an interpreter with him or hires one there.

Tursun's former colleague with the restaurant collected all his investments and emigrated to Canada with his family seven years ago. He tried to open a restaurant there, but the technical regulations and hygiene criteria are much higher than in China, and he had to divert his interests towards trade. However, Tursun's restaurant is of exemplary cleanliness. Every day, two hours before opening, all the employees take part in the general cleaning, and all the customers can see what transpires in the kitchen.

Another highly ranked value in Tursun's life is honesty. His employees are satisfied and faithful to him. "They are paid according to their experience and seniority. If I progress, they progress, too. We get along very well," claimed Tursun sincerely. He calculates the taxes without hiding anything and pays them accurately. "Why cheat the government? It would be cheating ourselves. We are all part of the government." He added, "Honest work, a quiet environment, and the hope of progress; one doesn't need anything more to be happy."

Every day Tursun lunches on *zhua fan* (*pol*^u*o* in Uyghur) at his restaurant. "For Uyghurs, a meal without *zhua fan* (rice with vegetables and sheep that one eats with the hands) is not a meal." That day I was his guest and he himself served me. A bowl of yogurt without sugar accompanied the meal. If one likes it sweet, sugar can be added; this is what the majority of Han do, as I noticed.

Then, we left the restaurant to go to his place. Tursun's apartment, on the 17th floor, was decorated with "a taste of Silk Road." Xinjiang is at the crossroads of great civilizations, the influence of which we can always feel: Islamic, Buddhist, Judeo-Christian, and Hindu. Travellers and merchants of the Middle East, India, China, and Europe met there.

Together with Tursun and his wife Dilaisam, who is from Korla in the Mongolian Autonomous Prefecture of Bayangol, a niece, and their 11-year-old granddaughter Parizat (which means "angel") live in the new apartment. Located in the downtown area, it cost – and this was expensive in 2004 – 2,600 yuan per sq m! But today, Tursun explained, the price exceeds 4,000 yuan per m. If in Beijing prices rise with the coming of the Olympic Games, in Urumqi, the rising costs are due to the stream of new inhabitants who flow from the rural areas and other provinces. It should be said that life is extremely pleasant in Urumqi: the sky is blue, trade flourishes, food production is abundant, and development opportunities abound.

Dilaisam, 55, retired recently. She doesn't feel bored at home, but complains that dust is present more often than not. She keeps busy with cooking and excels in pastry-making, as well as making sweets of all kinds. She used to knit often when she was young, but in the last five years, she found that buying ready-made woollen articles, even handmade ones, was cheaper. She sewed all of her clothing, using mostly the Uyghur silk called *ad'lais'* (*aideles, aidires, Atlas, Etles*). Moreover, she likes walking in the city by day and to watch TV in the evening very much.

26

Will the 2008 Olympic Games influence the development of Xinjiang and Tursun's business? He had not yet thought about that, Tursun admitted.

A JAUNT IN NATURE

As a human being doesn't live only to work, I had nothing on my schedule for Saturday, July 7. Nothing but a jaunt 40 km south of Urumqi, at the Banfang Pass (Banfanggou). As Xinjiang is crossed from west to east by three huge mountain ranges – Altay in the north, Tianshan in the middle and Kunlun in the south – passes are numerous in the region. Between these mountains lie the large basins of Junggar and Tarim. Urumqi is located at the south of the Junggar Basin and the north of the Tianshan Mounts.

In China, natural holiday resorts called *Dujiacun* open one after the other, and Xinjiang is no exception. We also see *Nongjiale*, meaning literally "Joy in a peasant home." In fact, some local provincial governments encourage and help the citizens to open their own homes

to tourists who will enjoy taking part in the farm work, cooking with the family, and appreciating a new experience for a few days.

We arrived around 12:00 – three cars and about 20 persons – in a very charming place. On the right, on the left, on the prairie and in the valley, we could see other holiday villages composed of yurts, the felt tents of the Asian nomads; we heard the children's laughter, and sometimes songs or instrumental music. Three kilometres away, on a high peak, a waterfall awaited admirers, but we preferred the whisper of the stream at the base of the mountain, the clucking of the naturally fed hens, and the greenery of the oat field. We immortalized these moments of happiness in photos.

We three curious women even entered incognito the earth's construction, where mushrooms were being grown. Plastic bags containing cotton balls with mushroom spores are placed directly on the soil; in the dark humidity, mushrooms develop and grow out of the bags.

It was a little too hot that day to play ping-pong,

badminton, or basketball, but what could be more enjoyable than riding a horse in the mountain then! And this is what we did, including the 74-year-old grandmother.

At meal time, typical Xinjiang dishes overflowed our table, one after the other: *dapanji* – a large plate of chicken pieces with bones, potatoes, and peppers; *zhua fan*, which

TURPAN AT 47 DEGREES CELSIUS

Turpan is a *Tujue** word (family of Altaic languages, including Uyghur) meaning "earth of abundance."

The little town is located 175 km southeast of Urumqi. In June, July, and August, the temperature is between 38 and 42 degrees. The maximum ever registered was 49.7° Celsius. It rains little and the water immediately feeds the underground sheet.

With only 600,000 habitants, Turpan seems empty. The population is 77 percent Uyghur, while the other

---

*The **Köktürks** or **Göktürks** (Blue Turks, meaning Celestial in Turkish), are known under the name of **Tujue** (突厥 tūjué) in Chinese. They established a powerful empire in 553 under the rule of Bumin Khan, which rapidly expanded all across Central Asia. They were the first people of the Turkish language to call themselves "Türk," meaning "strong," and the Chinese noun "tujue" probably comes from the plural türük.

23 percent are mostly Kazak, Hui, and Han, for a total of 36 ethnic groups. Except for a minority of Han, we were in a Muslim area.

It is in Turpan that the world's lowest depression can be found –Ayding Lake (or Aydingkol), meaning "moonlight" in Uyghur, at 154 m below sea level. Today, this dried-out lake and the sheet of salt that remains seem to be a reflection of the moon on the water or a large

mirror under the sun.

Turpan is the driest, warmest place in China. It is the dry climate that allowed the natural mummification of corpses buried at Astana or Gaochang (2,500 years ago for the oldest), as well as the preservation of the relics of ancient cities such as Jiaohe (Yerkoltu in Uyghur, which means cliff city), destroyed in 1383 by the Mongols, and others. The mummies were no longer where I saw them

in 1993, but in Turpan Museum. There are about 15, surprisingly well-preserved, among which are two couples and two babies.

The Jiaohe relics can be found 10 km west of Turpan, where no stream of water runs and not one herb trembles in the wind, and is of only one colour: sand. It was 47 degrees that day but the air being extremely dry made the heat bearable. It is difficult to imagine the shape of the old constructions when one looks at their ruins. However, an infant cemetery has been identified, but it is still unknown why 200 children were buried in a ground under the local government of the Huihu Period of Gaochang. The Jushi Kingdom was part of the Gaochang Uyghur Khanate more than 2,000 years ago.

One could believe that Turpan, where water is scarce and heat so intense, is totally arid, but ironically it is the paradise of the Hami melon. If Xinjiang produces the sweetest melons of the country, Turpan produces the sweetest of Xinjiang Autonomous Region. It also produces the sweetest grapes in the world. The grape dryers offer a unique image: isolated or grouped by four, five, or even hundreds, these sheds have walls containing as many holes as bricks, allowing the wind to circulate inside, between the bunches until the grapes are perfectly dry – resulting in a product for export that brings in a good income, along with Xinjiang cotton. If not all the

households grow melons, they all have a patio protected from the sun by a pergola.

My first image of Turpan: the triple row of trees planted on both sides of the streets. Children played in the canal. It was 13:00, the hottest time of the day, but the local population didn't seem to suffer from it. Mosques were numerous, various, and beautiful. And my first impression of cleanliness remained unchanged till the end.

My hotel was on the long and large pedestrian avenue paved with ceramic tiles, covered with a pergola where birds took their share of grapes.

Bezeklik means "where there are paintings"; it is in a valley of the Flaming Mountain, 60 km northeast of Turpan. Bezeklik is a suitable name for the Thousand Buddha Caves, where we can see that Xinjiang was Buddhist before adopting Islam in the 10th century under the Uyghur influence. In Turpan, we also find a rare testimony of Manichaeism, now an extinct religion, in the paintings of the grottoes and on the rocks of the Tuyu Valley.

A stop at the Dabancheng wind power plant was important for me because so many windmills presented a unique and impressive view. Who has not heard or hummed Wang Luobin's song, *The Girls of Dabancheng*? I will never know whether they are truly the most

beautiful girls because the wind blew them away! It is surely the ideal spot for windmills that spin at high speeds. If Xinjiang is rich in oil, it is also in clean energy – sun and wind energy – which are well-utilized.

Along the road, for kilometres and kilometres, we can see only stone desert or *gobi* desert. "Gobi" is a *Tujue* (Turkic) word meaning "where nothing grows easily" and is used in Chinese with this meaning. It should not be confused with the proper name Gobi Desert, which is also – obviously – a desert of *gobi*. Trees have been planted along the railway to protect it from being silted. In the 1960s, the train from Beijing started to reach

Urumqi; before, it ended at Hami, the most eastern city of Xinjiang; to go further, travellers used to hire a cart pulled by donkeys. These carts now are used as local taxis.

Yan Hu, or salt lake, is defined by its name, and is considered as a sea in the interior of Xinjiang.

The Flaming Mountain, "Huoyanshan" in Chinese, is located in the middle of the Turpan Depression, and is 98 km long and nine km wide. Its reddish colour is due to the oxidation of the stone, and the illusion of flame is strengthened by the vibration of the air over the stone which can be seen during the hottest hours of the day. A huge thermometer showed a soil temperature of 58°C at

19:00 that day.

In the surroundings of Turpan, sand and sunshine are used as a therapy. It is mostly the local people who bury their limbs in the burning sand containing iron ore, as a way to fight arthritis. Probably before long commercial establishments will take advantage of the opportunity offered by Mother Nature.

The road is of excellent quality its whole length. Five years ago, said the driver, it was built through thousands of sq km of desert. Far in the distance, I could see cement plant chimneys; elsewhere, an oil field.

The karez is an irrigation system unique to Xinjiang that can be seen especially in Turpan and Kumul ("Hami" in Chinese). Dug 2,000 years ago, it consists in vertical wells every 80 metres and linked by an underground canal 1.6 m high and 0.65 m wide, on a length between five

and 20 km. At the apogee of the system, in 1784, there were 172,367 wells for a total length of 5 272 km. Today, only 614 remain but the system still operates with the advantage that the underground water doesn't dry up, a considerable point in such a furnace.

Quickly before dinner, which is normally taken after 20:00, we visited the Sugong Minaret built in 1778 for Emin Hoja (*Hoja* means religious leader) by Emperor Qianlong in praise of his cooperation to the cause of the national unity by repelling the armed rebellion of the Junggar Uyghur aristocrats. It is the only minaret of totally Islamic style among hundreds in China. Non-Muslims and even women are now allowed to respectfully visit the mosque.

On the last day in this area, what could be more refreshing than a stroll in the Grape Valley? Since my first visit here 14 years ago, things had changed and the place was commercialized. I noticed that the kinds of grapes, fresh or dry, had not decreased. From the tiny black currants, as small as pepper grains, to the giant golden, orange or brown grapes, as big as Greek olives, there were at least 15 varieties.

GRANDMOTHER MELON

Wu Mingzhu, Han

W u Mingzhu is a small woman who doesn't show her 77 years. She moves with short, quick steps and speaks with a modulated voice of contained passion. She has an accent from the south. Who would have said that the melons that I have enjoyed since my arrival in Xinjiang were because of her!

Wu normally did not like to be interviewed, and she will speak about herself only if she is obliged to. That time, she willingly accepted my interview with the hope it could attract the interest of other countries to take up her cause – that of the Turpan melon. She asked that I go to her work place before 8:00, because the temperature was unbearable between 11:00 and 17:00. It was 45°C in Turfan on my arrival the day before; the morning of the interview, the sky was heavy, but as precipitations reach

only 18 mm per year, I knew it would probably not rain.

I thus found Wu Mingzhu already busy, under an immense metal structure with a pergola as a roof, choosing the melons that would be served at the end of the interview. When I started to ask her questions, she dismissed her staff so that we could speak in quieter surroundings.

Wu Mingzhu was born in 1930 in Wuhan, Hubei Province, to a father, a professor of English, and a mother, a nurse. Her only brother also became a teacher within the army. Her family lived in Nanjing, Jiangsu Province.

Agriculture as a subject of study was her own choice because, she said, her health was poor. Her father would

have preferred for her to go into engineering as she did very well in mathematics. At the age of 23, she earned her diploma from the Southwest Institute of Agriculture. In the 1930s, the Japanese invaded China and a large part of the population moved to flee from them. This is also what Wu Mingzhu's family did; they moved to Sichuan. When the danger was over, they went back to Nanjing, but Wu returned to Chongqing for her higher education.

Her four years of university left indelible marks. First, she learned from a Japanese professor that she herself should do one more step every day. All the students received 20 sq m of land that they should plough, sow, fatten, weed, and sprinkle themselves. "I do not have any merit," she said, "all my comrades cultivated this same spirit." Second, she was always imbued with the *leitmotiv* "to serve the people" (*wei renmin fuwu*). Twice she took part in a revolutionary campaign of agriculture. "We had to go to each family and help the household to achieve a task within a fixed time." Punctuality was an essential quality to become a member of the Party. Her teachers inculcated the idea of serving the people in the students, and Wu was so convinced of the importance of this point that she wrote in her diary, at the age of 21, that "this is the most beautiful thing in the world." Ever since childhood she wished to work in the countryside. At the end of her studies, the Institute proposed that the students choose areas of difficulty such as Yunnan, Guizhou, Sichuan, and 90 percent of them did it voluntarily. "Nobody was obliged to choose misery," she specified, "but it was to Xinjiang that I wanted to go, and my choice was accepted."

Not immediately, however. Wu first worked 10 months in Sichuan, then in Beijing for the Department of Rural Work of the CPC Central Committee for one and a half years. But it was very removed from her specialty and she did not intend to keep on doing clerical work. She wanted to exercise her skills on the ground in her specialty. In 1955, Xinjiang needed experts, mostly in agriculture, and this was the chance for Wu. The black-braided girl spent 15 days in a truck to reach Urumqi. There, she had to wait for her turn to be sent to Turpan and work the soil with her own hands.

The adaptation period did not prove to be easy but it was possible, since, 50 years later, Wu Mingzhu is still in the Turpan countryside, 183 km southeast of Urumqi.

The first difficulty lay in daily life. Wu had never eaten mutton meat and could not stand its smell. In Turpan, largely populated with Uyghurs and where she ate with the peasants, she had no choice. The first time, her stomach could not help rejecting what was imposed on it, and Wu cried. But she finally adapted and today she prefers mutton to pork. For sleeping, people lay down side-by-side on a large *kang* – a bed made of bricks heated by pipes passing underneath. She was given the best place, as an honoured guest, where the heat was most intense. "But it was also, by that fact, the place where fleas were more numerous," Wu remembered in a burst of laughter, adding that today, these people have much more comfortable houses than hers.

As for work, if the peasants cultivated corn, Wu had to help them and had no time left for her own research on melons. One day, after the harvest of the sorghum, her whole body ached so much that she could not move.

Heat was another major problem. Wu once harvested cotton at 48.1°C. In Turpan, the mercury passes 40°C 40 days a year. In 1958, while carrying her first child, Wu worked in the vineyards under such a heat wave, she remembered. There was no resting for the mother-to-be. In the evening, by the gleam of a candle, she could finally open her books and devote herself to her studies, at the cost of necessary sleep. In 1960, she walked for two days to find the ideal sweet melon, a *hongxincui*, which would become the ancestor of the favourite Turpan melon – a deep orange with firm and tender flesh. The temperature of the ground was then 81 degrees. Very happy with her discovery, Wu consumed the melon on the spot; it was enough to keep the seeds.

Fourth difficulty: language. Living among Uyghurs,

Wu had to gradually learn their language. In the beginning, because of her bad pronunciation, when one asked her the time and she answered, for example, "Nine o'clock," they all made fun of her. What she had said was something like "nine men." However, the Uyghurs quickly adopted her and gave her a name with a touch of tenderness: Ayimuhan (Moon Girl).

What about family relations? When Wu was named to go to Xinjiang, she first went back to Nanjing to say farewell to her family. All were very happy to see her because they had been waiting for a long time. When she announced her destination so far from home, the smiles changed into reproaches; nobody agreed. Wu had already undergone a surgical operation and they argued that her health would be subjected to too hard a test. She held her position and allowed her mother to accompany her to the station under the condition that there would be no tears. However, her mother was confined to her bed for three days after her daughter left.

Ten days after the birth of Wu's son, her mother arrived in Xinjiang to help her. Three months later, the grandmother took the baby back to Nanjing, where he grew up without ever seeing his mother. Wu's daughter was then born in Nanjing. When the baby reached "100 days" (a special age for the Chinese), Wu returned to Turpan, leaving her child who had started calling her aunt

"Mom." This girl, now married, says that her mother never once changed her diaper. Wu's work place had suggested that she bring her children to Turpan, but Wu answered that she could not maintain an excellent standard of work while caring for two children. Wu Mingzhu didn't attend either of her children's weddings. She admitted, laughingly, but it seemed that she spoke from the heart: "I like my melons more than I like my children."

The woman of science said she succeeded, thanks to support from five sources. First, the support of the neighbourhood farmers. In spring 1957, she and a team of people went to attend training on the culture of melons. One day, she decided to return to Turpan for personal reasons and left without telling anyone. They were all extremely worried, and after a sleepless night, the whole group left to search for her. When they found her, they cried tears of joy. Support also came from the authorities: the directors of the Institute helped her with her research and studies, and the government of the Xinjiang Uyghur Autonomous Region provided her with the necessary equipment and facilities. Other countries, including the United States with which collaboration is very enriching, and Japan, receive Wu's students for their doctorate degrees. Experience and the fruit of research are shared. The United States taught Wu, who goes there often, as to Israel and Japan, to treat a melon disease.

The research funds come only from China: Xinjiang in the beginning, then the Hami Research Centre on Melon under the Academy of Agricultural Sciences of Xinjiang. With Taiwan and Shanghai also there is close cooperation. "Grandmother Melon," as the Uyghurs call her, went back and forth between Xinjiang and Hainan for years "because the conditions of research offered by this insular province were favourable," she explained. Wu emphasized the support from her immediate collaborators, her colleagues, and disciples. Nevertheless, Wu has one regret: neglecting her husband, without whom she would never have made a success of her career.

Yang Qiyou arrived at Xinjiang in 1956, leaving behind his university in Jiangsu to follow his wife. He started teaching at the Urumqi University. Wu did not cook; he did. He even took the meals to her work place. "He took care of me more than I did of him," she confessed, "and he shared the work of the farmers to support me." In 1982, as his health declined without apparent reason, Yang returned to Jiangsu but Wu did not follow him. It was stomach cancer, and the disease became fatal in 1986. When his wife asked him whether it was because of her he had gone to Xinjiang, he denied it, adding that it was his own choice. He had taught four years in Nanjing but 20 in Urumqi, without a chance of promotion or title. "He had only these two words: *feng*

xian ('devotion' in English)," Wu stated. I did not dare ask her whether she would live the same life if she could start again, because I supposed that one never disavows a choice made with passion. After Yang Qiyou's death, Wu returned to Xinjiang – which she made her motherland – with the intention of working as hard as two people. She lives simply, and eats and dresses soberly.

I suspected that Wu had received some honours during her half-century career. Through questions and prompting, I ended up knowing that her greater honour consisted in becoming a member of the Chinese Communist Party in 1953; her eyes shone with pride when she told me that. In the 1980s, she received the "March Eighth" (*San Ba*) Prize created by Mao Zedong for the women, then the Prize of Special Contribution of Youth; she was appointed "Model Worker" and "Hard-Working Avant-Garde." A grant of 100 yuan per month for life to the "Young Researcher" was allotted to her. Wu saw her name on the list of the "Ten Elite People" of China. In 1999, she was named academician of the Chinese Academy of Engineering. A national prize of Scientific Work in 2003, a scientific prize of Progress and the appointment of Model Worker of Ethnic Groups were also allotted to her, and probably others. In which year? She didn't remember, she said....

According to Shi Huiqiong, director of the Turpan

Information Office, if Wu is rooted in Xinjiang, it is first because she absolutely wanted to make her speciality profitable, and then because she felt the misery of the peasants at that difficult time and wanted to help them get rid of poverty. She often had opportunities to go to teach or continue her research in other countries, but always refused. What if a post of vice mayor were offered to her? She thinks, 'I'm much more useful to my melons.'

Presently, Wu Mingzhu has two wishes: one is to see the *hamigua* – the Hami melons – enter the market and for the farmers to become wealthy; the other is that her disciples surpass her in researching melons.

Xinjiang cultivates 101 kinds of melons; Turpan, 40, including 30 new kinds borne from the efforts of Wu and her team. It may seem easy to access the market, but there are still many problems to be solved beforehand. For example, it is necessary to develop a thinner bark to decrease the weight, but a bark strong enough to resist the movements of transportation; to develop melons that last till the winter; to develop melons that are small enough to be consumed in one sitting; and even to develop melons that are "nice to look at," the woman of science explained.

In order to improve the soil, Wu grows onions close to the melon seedlings. She explained the "watering by dripping" technique to me, another of her experiments.

When we returned under the large tent, I found young women busy sorting, classifying, and packing seeds.

Then we proceeded to a "scientific" tasting of melons: each one was numbered, weighed, and registered. Samples of the three kinds I showed preference for was discreetly put in the car to take back, without my knowledge.

Speaking about bark, I was sorry to see such waste. Wu answered that a great deal of the bark is used to feed the sheep; for the remainder, there are other possible uses but this field of research belongs to other scientists. Her field covers the improvement of species and varieties: melons with various degrees of sugar, even completely acidic; melons with apple or pineapple taste; melons with or without seeds; melons that are yellow, green, white, red; melons that are striped, smooth, or "embroidered";

melons that are grown ground-free; and even melons that
are the result of seeds that have spent a month in
interplanetary space. These last ones are already in their
third generation.

Last, I learned a secret that I will pass on to you. The
watermelon, which is especially aqueous, is Yin (female)
and the *tiangua*, sweet melon, is Yang (male). Therefore,
while consuming only part of the fruit, the higher part
of watermelon and the lower part of Hami melon are
tastier.

I thought that *hamigua* would be everywhere in
Hami; it is in Turpan that I saw tight rows of stalls along
the streets.

IN THE HEART OF EMBROIDERY

Ajiahan·Sahmet, Uyghur

Belonging to the sixth generation of embroiderers, Ajiahan has become a symbol of this art. She learned embroidery from her mother at the age of 13. When I arrived at her place in Shazaojing, a village of Kumul ("Hami" in Chinese), the sun penetrated the smallest crevices, and anything that could shine shined in the large room where Ajiahan assembled her works and trophies.

In this village of 1,818 inhabitants, 98 percent are Uyghur. Ajiahan was born in 1952 to an agricultural family. She attended compulsory school – primary and middle school. She understood Chinese better than she spoke it, but we needed an interpreter – a young woman who also practices embroidery.

Ajiahan's mother was also a famous embroiderer, but

her daughter surpassed her, especially by marketing her work. Since 1985, Ajiahan has often been invited to give demonstrations or to teach in various places around the country. "I don't like to move," she said, "and I don't even have time." Ajiahan is a wife and a mother, and she has made a point of continuing her career without neglecting these aspects of her life. Even during the great Sino-Japanese Exhibition of farmer paintings held in Beijing in 1988, "my works went there, but not me," said Ajiahan, who also paints, in a burst of laughter. Her absence didn't prevent her from winning first prize with *Spring Labor*, which is an homage to the abolition of the agricultural commune system and to the privatization of the land.

I politely asked to see this work of about one sq m. She didn't have it anymore; not even a photograph. It remained in Beijing. She could only show me its draft and the trophy it won. Ajiahan has accumulated eight

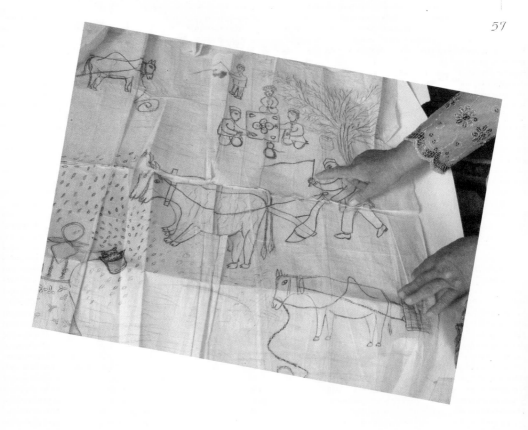

prizes up to now.

Self-taught like the majority of the peasant painters, Ajiahan also practices the art of paper-cutting. However, for her, paper-cutting is only one of the preparatory stages of her embroidery, as models to be transferred on fabric before stitching. She creates her exclusive models which require several starts, because correction is impossible. "If I make a mistake, I must throw the piece out and start over again," she said.

Ajiahan drew from between the pages of a large book her best paper-cut models, 20 or 25. Some were ruffled, others folded. She thought of publishing them in a catalogue for posterity. While I was spreading them out to take a photo, Ajiahan confided in me that she usually didn't show them to journalists. For me, she had made an exception. That was what it meant to come from afar!

On this subject, I would like to relate an anecdote. In Beijing where I have been living for more than 16 years, I very often pass for a Uyghur. The most astonishing thing is that the Uyghurs themselves think I am one of theirs. When I say jokingly to the Han that I am Uyghur, no one ever doubts me. In Xinjiang, for two weeks, I travelled in the company of the Han; however, it is I that the Uyghur police officer addressed, in "our" language, to explain why the traffic was blocked. Another day, when my Han driver asked for the way, the Uyghur

passer-by who didn't speak Chinese fluently changed languages as soon as he saw me in the car and addressed his explanation to me.

Another Ajiahan's work that won a prize is the *Cockfight*, a favourite entertainment of the Uyghur people. The artist surprised me by her perspicacity and especially her audacity in a painting done in 1992. *The Back Door* is a multidimensional work showing a man bribing for favours, and is also a critic of piracy and fraud. At that time, the local authorities believed it preferable not to expose such a critical painting, but, today, China is opened and citizens can express themselves more freely. To paint the *Mosque*, the artist had to return to the spot 15 times because then, women could not enter mosques and there were always missing details that she had not sufficiently observed.

Among Ajiahan's collection was a large, silk crepe shawl that she kept despite the rips, and another one that she planned to do again, she said, because the silk was not of good enough quality. There was also a very old *doppa* embroidered by one of her ancestors, but she didn't know who wore it. I found the *doppa*s on the rack very attractive, and I decided that it was time for me to get one, since it was my third visit to Xinjiang. *Doppa* means "daily life necessity." Ajiahan showed me the differences between those for men and those for women, and, as she wanted to offer me a gift, she invited me to choose one I liked.

Since entering her place, I looked at Ajiahan's work with a question in my mind. Was her inspiration of Han style? She reproduced peonies and lotuses, not arabesques, Arabic inscriptions, ogival windows, moon crescents or other Islamic or Uyghur figures like those of the *adlai* silk. As there were no Han embroiderers in this area to

influence her, I asked her why. She couldn't answer, and seemed not to really understand what I was talking about. I didn't persist. But upon returning to Beijing, I continued my research to learn that the embroidery of *doppa* varies with the areas: Hotan, Kashgar, Kuqa, and Turpan, and that the Hami style is comparatively complex, colorful, bright, and showy.

When I asked Ajiahan what was the greatest difficulty of her craft, she answered that it was the fact that her son who graduated in computer science could not find a job. He since had tried to find employment through the

Internet. Her three daughters were all university graduates but only one had a job; the other two worked with their mother. Obviously we had a linguistic problem. I phrased my question differently: Is embroidery difficult on the eyes? Ajiahan, who didn't wear glasses, said that it was not. When she was young, she liked to embroider very much, even at night, but her parents forbade it to save lamp oil. Her only problem currently is arthritis in her hands, which prevented her from working for several weeks in recent years.

Ajiahan is a very active businesswoman. In 2004, she had 66 students and, in 2007, 116. Presently she hires 30 women between the ages of 23 and 70 years – all village

women who work mostly at home. But every day, some of them come to Ajiahan to get some work or bring back what they have finished. They are people who have lost their employment or widows, and five physically disabled persons, including four mute-and-deaf people. They learn from Ajiahan, who provides them with thread and fabric; when they successfully complete a piece, Ajiahan buys it from them and uses these embroideries as components of large works.

Business is growing. Ajiahan has already created her trademark, which is known in all of Xinjiang, and is beginning to be known in all of China and even abroad. Exporting will begin to Turkey, and perhaps Japan. This is why Ajiahan presently invests in building a series of seven small workshops with specialized functions, side-by-side, which will form a factory of almost 1,000 sq m altogether. From the money this good-hearted woman earns, a portion is used for that construction, another for helping needy students, orphans, etc.

Embroidery requires an important investment: fabric, thread, and ornaments. Ajiahan buys 20,000 yuan of thread every two months. The paper used as support in *doppa* making, for instance, comes from cement bags, which cost two yuan each. This paper called "cow skin" has become difficult to find now that polythene is used for packing.

Mohammed, Ajiahan's husband, retired after a career of 34 years as a high school teacher. He has cultivated a piece of land between the house and the workshops-to-be and raises four or five sheep, hens, and a donkey.

Ajiahan would not let me leave without having some tea. Calling it *hulucha*, she poured it from a gourd that keeps it fresh. On the immense *kang* Mohammed prepared large plates of watermelon, sweet melons, and Hami jujubes, all local specialties.

Later, at the restaurant, the waiter still addressed me in the Uyghur language, all the more reason that I proudly wore my *doppa*, souvenir of Ajiahan.

PEAKS REACHING THE SKY

Wang Tienan, Han

He lives in Urumqi, close to the Xinjiang University. Sun-tanned but not excessively, Wang Tienan exudes good health. There is a reason, as we will see. I arrived at his place at 11:00. In Xinjiang, people generally start to work at 9:30 or 10:00 till 14:00, and from 16:00 to 18:00 or later in the afternoon. In several houses and offices, there are two clocks: one indicates Beijing time, that of the whole country; the other, the local time, or two hours less. Meals are generally taken at 8:00, 14:00, and 21:00.

In the small studio where a computer and bookshelves are installed, my eye was caught by some photographs: the great moments of Wang's alpinist life. There was also a very old climber pick with a wooden handle. Three pairs of skis – of the latest fashion – leaned against the wall; the couple and their son practice this sport. As it was the season, 10 watermelons and several Hami melons were aligned along the wall, trying to make themselves as discreet as possible.

Wang was born in November 1956 in Changchun, Jilin Province. He was one year old when his parents moved to Xinjiang. His father was a specialist in contagious animal diseases, and his mother, a nurse. They came to help Xinjiang to develop, and remained, like the majority of like people who arrived during the same period. Wang's wife, Cheng Zhanxiang, comes from a Hunan family. When her parents came to Xinjiang in 1961, serving the same cause, her mother was six months pregnant. Cheng was thus born in Xinjiang. As soon as we started to converse, I intuited that she had been born within an army family; I was right. I also had the feeling that she was a professor. In fact, she and I were both high school teachers.

When Wang Tienan completed his high school studies in 1975, it was one year before the end of the "cultural revolution." The young "intellectuals" were sent to be re-educated by the peasants, and Wang was sent to the Tianshan Mountains. He then found interest in vast spaces and mountains. In 1977, he was admitted to the faculty of physics of Normal University of Xinjiang. Once he became an engineer, he has always worked and

still works with the Xinjiang University of Television. After teaching for 10 years, he now works as a controller of the Internet technology system of this establishment.

It is only in 1989 that Wang undertook his first mountain climbing expedition, a three-day excursion to the top of 3,650 m Tianshan, with a slope of 90 km. Not only the height of a peak but its slope, soft or difficult, accounts for much of the degree of difficulty and danger. Before the 1990s, Wang Tienan explored mostly deserts. To date, he has climbed several peaks of Tianshan and Kunlun mountains – places where very few have left their traces. He finds the Altay Mountains, the more northern ranges of the country, less interesting because they offer fewer challenges. The duration of the excursions varies from five days to one, two, or three months. Sometimes Wang leaves alone, sometimes with friends, and sometimes he acts as a guide. The heights of the conquered peaks reach 3,650 m, 4,480 m or 5,180 m, and the covered distance from 60 to 900 km. The groups number between five and 40 participants.

In 1998, Wang Tienan was the first Chinese person to reach the summit of the Bogda, the main peak of Tianshan Mountains. A Japanese mountaineer had accomplished the feat in 1981.

The year 1999 was special for mountaineer Wang, and one climbing excursion is worth telling in detail.

Photo provided by Wang Tienan

On July 3, the Mustaghata (Muztagh Ata, or father of the glaciers) team of 15 members started towards the summit of 7,546 m. On July 8, the mountaineers set up their camp at 4,300 m. Twelve days later, at 7:30 on the 20th, they reached 6,700 m. At 30°C below zero, they climbed during more than seven hours before finally reaching, at 14:40, the summit.

To date, Wang has climbed the Bogda five times. He has crossed the Taklimakan Desert, which name means "Sea of Death"; it is the third largest desert in the world after the Sahara and the Kalahari. There are some 40 m height dunes. Temperature varies from 40°C below zero in winter to 50°C in summer. Such a climate doesn't allow any life! In 1992, Wang and a team of Japanese people crossed it from west to east – 900 km – in three months.

The peaks that Wang prefers are those requiring technique; the most difficult, in fact. But the most difficult are also the most dangerous. "Two threats lie in wait for the mountaineer. First, winds of sand: at midday it is as dark as night. During an excursion with 200 camels, we undertook such a wind, which cost the lives of 130 camels." I was astonished that so many animals perished but no man. "Camels are tall," said Wang, "and cannot hide in holes; moreover, they transport the material and they are exhausted." The other threat is the fault hidden under a layer of virgin snow. "If you fall in it, you remain there."

"What about avalanches?"

"Yes, but they are less frequent and often foreseeable," the alpinist answered. "Once, while climbing down from a peak, we met three Hong Kong people going up. We

Photo provided by Wang Tienan

exchanged some words. But they have never come down…. There is also a Japanese man who died on the mountain; we found his body." Wang Tienan himself almost left his life behind in the mountain several times. He told of a mishap: one day he was climbing alone and stopped at an altitude of 6,800 m and chatted with two Frenchmen who were settling in for the night. He was tired and would have liked to sleep in their tent, but it was too small. He set out again, alone, in the darkness, and fell into a fault. At five meters deep, he found purchase. To avoid slipping even more, he hung on and decided to wait for the morning light before trying to hoist himself up. What he feared more was falling asleep. It would have been certain death; at -15°C, freezing is fatal. During the eight hours, he unceasingly moved his hands and feet. At dawn, he succeeded in coming out of the fault and once the fog dissipated, he noticed that he had almost reached the goal: at 200 meters.

Wang Tienan is president of Urumqi Association of Mountaineering and Exploration (with approximately 80 members) since the death of the former president who occupied the post only one year. This is how his passing happened. In 2001, Dong Wuxin, a good friend of Wang, took part in an expedition on the Silk Road at the south of the Tianshan Mountains. When he saw a stone that reminded him the shape of a funerary stele, Dong wrote on the smooth surface *Wu Ming Mu* (*Tomb of the Unknown*). Beside the stone Dong placed a horse skull bleached by the wind on which he traced: *Dong Xia* (*Dong the Strong*). Two days later, at the crossing of a fast water stream, Dong fell in the water. With cables, his companions could have saved him, perhaps, but they had left the cables in the vehicle. They all saw him losing his balance, then struggling, and finally being swallowed by the floods. Impossible to catch Dong physically, Wang captured him on film by photographing his drifting body. It was only three months later that the second research team, in which Wang Tienan took part, could find Dong's remains. In the summer of 2002, Wang went back to spread Dong's ashes among his beloved mountains. He will never forget this scene.

Photo provided by Wang Tienan

At Wang Tienan's place, the environment was warm and the house was always full of friends. In fact, during this interview, three people, mountaineers, came. His son also telephoned. He was 21 years old and a sophomore in Kazakhstan where he studied Russian. Back in China for the holidays, he was climbing the Mustaghata, heading a group of 38, including two Tibetans. On the phone, his father advised him to slow down. He was young and in good health, but the climbing of 4,000 m from Kashgar had been much too fast, according to the expert. "One should spend 20 days to reach this top, though it is possible to make it in 10 days," explained Wang Tienan, hanging up the phone and returning to our conversation as if nothing had interrupted it. He didn't worry about

his son, whom he had trained from his childhood. At the age of 13, the young man, who was 1.80 m, accompanied his father to the top of the Bogda.

As for Wang's wife, she doesn't worry either when her husband leaves for an expedition. The short wave radio keeps them in contact. But when news comes after two or three days of silence, she feels relieved.

"The Chinese started mountaineering rather late," said Wang, "and the first groups came mainly from Beijing, Guangzhou, and Shenzhen. But in the last two years, there are people from Zhejiang and Fujian who come to climb our mountains in Xinjiang."

Wang Tienan would like to climb the Alps and other famous peaks of the world, but it is very expensive, taking into account permits, local guides, and carriers; in short, two dozen people, and animals. The equipment is heavy and numerous. Each mountaineer requires four bottles of oxygen. And tents. And food. A cook is needed, too. All these people must be paid. The Qomolangma is also expensive: 200,000 yuan per team. Five members of the Urumqi Association of Mountaineering and Exploration went there in May after preparing for two months. Wang was not part of it, but he went to Tibet to encourage the climbers. Bad luck for him: his motorcycle slipped and his right knee was seriously wounded. He would undergo the second surgery in a few days.

What do people do with the empty bottles of oxygen? My question made Wang smile; he shook his head. "Pollution. You want to talk about pollution of Qomolangma? We leave everything on the spot, including the old tents that we will not use anymore.

Teams of volunteers are required to collect waste, an unimaginable quantity! Mountaineers are very numerous now; they have to queue up for their turn to go up."

To satisfy an old curiosity, I enquired: "How can the team leader climb as there are not yet cables in position?"

"The leader uses a peak and nails to open the way. He is the one who installs the cables for the following climbers. Certain peaks are very high but do not require cables; sometimes one needs 3,500 m of cord; one pulls up the cable and starts again and again, five or six times."

At home, Wang likes to read, especially in the data processing field. He has written four books on alpinism and a great number of articles.

According to Wang, there are two kinds of mountain lovers: those who climb until old age comes to remove their means; and those who die in the mountains. "Alpinism is not a hobby, it is a way of life," Wang said. Sometimes Wang is very busy and feels the pressure of life, but he knows that a mountain is awaiting him, and this is enough to endure anything.

SELF-TAUGHT
AND HUMANIST

Liu Yulian, Han

In 1966, Liu Yulian, then 17 years old, arrived from Gansu with her father to settle in Erpu, a village of the Kumul (Hami) Prefecture where the population is

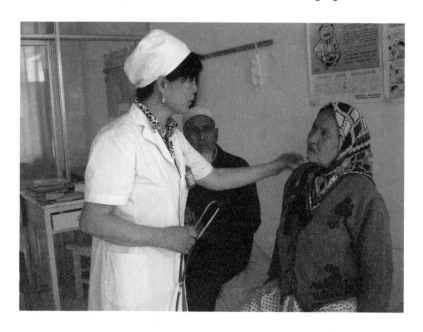

98 percent Uyghur.

She had no intellectual luggage except her middle school diploma. On her arrival, the local government chose her because of her instruction – a valid level at that time – to work at the local medical station. She knew nothing about medicine and was sent in June 1971 to take a three-month course in an army hospital. Famous medical officers taught her acupuncture, she remembered. In the evenings, the young woman practiced inserting needles on herself. Returning to the village, she heard about an arthritic man who had tried all kinds of treatments without any results. Liu offered to try acupuncture on him. With nothing to lose, he agreed, and the results were positive.

One day, Liu visited an old lady suffering from a very bad headache. In fact, the patient had a fever of 40.4 degrees. It would have been better to go to the hospital, but the patient protested because she couldn't afford it. Liu Yulian sought a solution in books and found that aspirin could help. The fever dropped and the patient needed no other treatment.

How could Erpu people not like Liu Yulian? Her name soon became "Yatou," which means "the girl." First, because the patient cured by her good care ceaselessly praised the Yatou's merits and also because her Chinese name was difficult to remember for the Uyghurs, who

preferred to call her simply "the girl."

When she started to work, Liu saw and understood the misery of the village inhabitants and decided to do something for them. It didn't take long to appreciate her kindness and her soft character. The biggest obstacle was verbal communication. The population is almost completely Uyghur and Liu is Han. Even today the village counts 1,079 inhabitants among 320 households, including only five Han households.

This difficulty did not deter Liu, who started to ardently study the language – oral and written. Today, she understands and speaks Uyghur just like the local population, and can read and write what is necessary for her work, albeit slowly.

Liu Yulian has kept a strong Gansu accent. Why did she come from Gansu to Xinjiang? "The 'cultural revolution' had started. My father was about to be made an object of criticism, so my uncle who worked with the railways said to him: 'Come with me to Hami.' My father asked me whether I wanted to accompany him. Once here, we came to realize that he would no longer be publicly criticized. I thought he would go back to Lanzhou, but he said: 'We are fine here, and Xinjiang is also China. So, I'll remain.' My mother came later."

Why not rather help the poor of Gansu? I asked the self-educated "doctor." The 100,000 Chinese who came from the whole country in 1954 within the framework of the Production & Construction Corps to help Xinjiang develop settled in their new homeland and assimilated into the population. Very few left, and a great many of those who did regretted doing so after a while and returned: they had from then on new roots.

A village doctor earned between 20 to 30 yuan a month. It was an appreciable income at that time. But who would have said that more than 40 years later, Liu Yulian's monthly allowance would still be only 350 yuan? Liu has no insurance, no retirement funds. Her colleague is a graduate nurse who earns reasonable wages. Each village has at least one medical station, and it is compulsory that two people are on hand. Liu harbored no jealousy but she noticed the inequity. Not only did she not complain, she said she was very happy. She liked her work and especially the people to whom she has dedicated her life.

No holidays, festive days, or weekends for Liu. In the evening, she read and studied medicine. Through the years, she took other training courses and exams. She watched little TV because, she said, due to aging, her sight has declined. However, she did not wear glasses. Is it vanity? Liu is a very beautiful woman who didn't show her age; she wore a row of pearls and earrings with her white uniform. Questioned about her own health, she

answered that she felt pain in her renal area and arthritis in her knees; would this be the consequence of her high heels? She ate little and irregularly, she admitted, which might have been the cause of her stomach problems. However, she did not look after herself nor would she consult specialists.

For four decades, Liu has devoted herself to her patients. "She doesn't know the difference between day and night when it comes to service," said Wu Zhengyi, her husband. Patients who have no money? She doesn't care. It is free for the poor. A "thank you" is enough for Liu, and the fact that people rely on her fills her heart with satisfaction. Even more, she has already spent 35,000 yuan on her patients and 6,000 to help needy students pursue their studies.

Without a diploma in medicine, Liu Yulian is not authorized to perform all the medical procedures. However, could she specialize in gynaecology, geriatrics, and pediatry at the same time? When a case exceeds her abilities, she sends the patient to consult at Hami Hospital.

"Do you practice preventive medicine?" I asked. She did not seem to understand my question. I specified that health starts with personal hygiene.

"Yes," she said, "I tell people to take care of cleanliness."

In the locality, the major affliction for a long time was goitre. At 40, the locals started to exhibit symptoms. Liu didn't really research it, but she asked herself what could be the cause of so many incidences, and found an iodine deficiency. She thus advised the villagers to consume iodized salt. I know that, in certain places, the local government provides iodized salt. Liu said that the Erpu inhabitants buy it themselves on the market. The disease regressed significantly and is almost eradicated.

Liu married Wu Zhengyi in 1969, "perhaps," said Wu, who forgot the year, while the woman corrected him: 1967. The couple live "together" very little, although they share the same roof. Even the meals are seldom eaten together. In the morning, Liu swallows the breakfast her husband prepares and leaves immediately for work. Wu washes the dishes and cleans up before leaving to do his farmer's work. He has 14 *mu* (15 *mu* = 1 ha) of land dispersed in three places, on which he cultivates mostly cotton. Behind the house, a kitchen garden is enough for the couple's needs. When he goes back home, Wu finds neither woman nor dinner. He starts to cook and waits for Liu. Sometimes he suggests that she give up her work, which does not bring anything back into the home and to stay at home. Not only could he provide for their needs but with two people working the land, they could cultivate more land and raise more animals.

A few years ago, at Spring Festival time – the Lunar
New Year and the most important festival of the year
for the Chinese – Wu found the house empty. People
came from everywhere to offer their wishes, but Liu was
invisible. Wu waited for his wife for so long that, in the
end, he dined alone. When she finally returned, he was
not in a mood to welcome her and said: "Why don't you
take your belongings and move to the medical station?"
Touched by his outburst of emotion, Liu decided to make
an effort. One evening, she returned early and they both
prepared the meal together. "Like a real family,"
remembered Wu, patiently. "She is like that, who could
change her?" he smiled, shaking his head.

In such a situation, what is the meaning of marriage?

I asked Liu if, at the time she married, she intended to have a "real" family, with children. She admitted that she never thought about it. She and her husband grew up together. She was a very pretty girl, and Liu's family was financially comfortable. Her parents arranged the marriage and gave her to Wu.

On December 16, 1969, Liu, then eight months pregnant, received patients until late afternoon despite strong abdominal pains. At 22:00 that evening, she gave birth to her first daughter who lived for only half an hour. Instead of taking the rest necessary to her own health, Liu returned to work 10 days later. She was needed! A second pregnancy occurred, then a third, ending in early miscarriages or death of the baby shortly afterwards. A baby girl lived 10 months. Finally, she had triplets: three girls who survived only a few days, said Liu, adding with tears in her eyes, "I gave birth to seven children and only my son is still alive." While Liu still had milk following the birth of her triplets, a girl was born to a Hui family and the parents – too poor – had to give the baby away. Liu's mother-in-law sought the child and brought her to her daughter-in-law, who adopted her. Ethnically speaking, Hui people are Islamic-Han. When Xiao Ying reached three years of age, Liu Yulian got pregnant again. That time, things were fine.

Who raised her children as she and her husband were

very busy and had no assistance? Liu said that after having fed her daughter and son their breakfast and having made them relieve themselves, she lay them down on the low table, which was on the *kang*, and tied them to prevent them from falling or running outside. From time to time, she would return home to check whether things were normal.

Despite multiple miscarriages, Liu continued to work more than was reasonable. Only "her" patients mattered. She rarely saw her father and mother, two sisters, and two brothers; there was no time for them because her village required her. One day in October 1986, her younger sister came to tell her that their mother felt bad, very bad. Liu Yulian went to see her mother, but her treatment had no effect. She said to her sister that the next day she would take their mother to Hami Hospital for a check up. However, the next morning she suddenly remembered that she had to give an injection to a child. Liu waited, but the patient didn't show up. However, other patients did, which made her completely forget her mother who was still waiting. Her sister reprimanded her, "Our father has already died; do you want us to live without a mother now?" Liu Yulian was deeply moved. She replied that she had to look after a child first and that she would see her mother immediately after. But five days passed before she found time to go to the hospital, where she was then told that her mother had terminal stomach cancer. The mother died one month later. Liu was sorry, but what would have happened to her patients if she had not looked after them?

On May 14, 2007, a long interview of Liu Yulian appeared in the *Hami Journal*. The journalists had requested the impressions of Liu's family on her attitude and behavior. Her adoptive daughter said that her mother had "never" been free. In spring 2000, Xiao Ying gave birth to a girl. The grandmother saw her granddaughter 10 times up till the interview. At the medical station where her mother works, seeing the promiscuity and misery, Xiao Ying was nauseated. I must say that two

years ago, a new clinic worthy of this name, large and clean, has been built. According to Liu's daughter, no one in the family approved of the life Liu carries out. Her son, a worker for an oil company, compared his mother with a clock that never stops. Liu's daughter-in-law underwent a caesarean four years ago; she spent 50 days in convalescence and her mother-in-law visited her only once for an hour or two. In four years, the grandson hasn't spent 10 days with his grandmother.

Four times the medical station has been robbed. Each time, Liu borrowed money from her family to put it back into operation as soon as possible. In 2001, her husband and his father bought a minibus they used as a shuttle between Erpu and Hami. The businesses continued till the fourth burglary: Liu immediately needed 16,000 yuan, which required selling the vehicle to refurnish the clinic.

After this interview at the clinic which was conducted while patients walked in and out, Liu was going home for lunch and invited me. With a half smile, I asked, "Aren't you a woman who doesn't cook?" She made a point of making me the honoured guest of the house and added, "I can cook when I want to." She lived in a mud house. I noticed that in Xinjiang, adobe was rare. A broad pergola threw a little shade in front of the door. The sun of Erpu was so dazzling that the eyes couldn't stay open.

Inside, three large rooms were in perfect order. In the room where I was invited to enter was a huge *kang*. Liu's husband sliced watermelons and sweet melons for me. The juice of the fruits inevitably dripped on the beaten earth, which absorbed it. On the table the first grapes of the season and dried Hami jujubes soon arrived.

Liu became a member of the Party in 1986. As I looked at a certificate allotted to "Comrade Liu Yulian" by the Communist Party in June 2007, she deposited on the *kang* a suitcase containing at least 30 prizes and recognitions from various sources and levels.

As the last question, I asked Liu Yulian if she had any regret or a wish. She regretted not having been able to attend university. The eldest of five children, if she had continued to study, as her parents would have liked her to, money would not have been sufficient to send the younger ones to school. In the end, she preferred working so that each one could have his or her share. What she hoped most ardently that day was to always better her work so that Erpu progresses and that its inhabitants can have an easier and pleasant life.

A LIFE FOR A TREASURE

Zhou Ji, Han

When I reminded him of our appointment the day before, he seemed a little confused. Had he forgotten? Had he taken another engagement? He reassured me, "I am a little busy but I will not postpone our appointment. Can you be there at 10:30?" I was there, but he was not. I waited patiently till he entered the hall of the World Plaza Hotel at a fast pace, without even glancing around at the people awaiting others. I recognized him: the perfect image that I had made of him in my mind and the resemblance to Wang Luobin. What do these two Han men have in common? They both dedicated their lives to the development and propagation of the Xinjiang music.

Zhou Ji is 64 years old. Despite his one-hour delay due to multiple simultaneous occupations, he did not

express any trouble being the subject of an interview and asked me to follow him. I believed that he was taking me to a quieter room, but to my great surprise, when he opened the door of the hall, I saw about 50 persons – men, women and children – in theatrical costumes, musical instruments in hand, sitting or standing, repeating

their parts. A great show was under preparation for the evening and Zhou Ji was at the same time cultural advisor, director of the artists, and master of ceremonies.

We sat at a table and I started to ask questions less about himself than on Muqam which has been his research subject for 40 years. He answered with an absolute focus, stopping sometimes to give instructions or to solve a problem on which one came to consult him.

Muqam is an Arabic word meaning classical music or oral tradition. In Xinjiang, the "Twelve Muqam" refer to the major "systems" specific to the places where there is a form of Muqam. This music and its interpretation vary according to places and include a large part of improvisation although the basic texts and music are written. Thus there are Kashgar Muqam, Hotan, Aksu, Ili, Hami, Daolang Muqam, etc. However, the territory of this particular art exceeds the Chinese borders and it can be found elsewhere in Asia, Middle East, Europe and Africa in countries and regions such as India, Cashmere, Pakistan, Iran, Iraq, Russia, Turkey, Libya, Morocco, Mauritania, Egypt, Syria, Algeria, and Tunisia: 19 in all, each one in its own language and each one under a different name. The word Muqam indicates only Xinjiang Muqam. Nobody knows where and when Muqam started. It is in China that we find the longest: a complete "opera" lasts several hours or even days.

I better understand Muqam after having listened to Professor Zhou's explanations. There are three types of Muqam. *Qiongnagemam* constitutes a show of one hour. It used to be presented in private houses of affluent people. The actors use dance and music as their means of expression. It is the most difficult part, and only a singer who can interpret it can be called a specialist, because the text is in "chaktai" (archaic Uyghur). Was it transmitted from mouth to ear? "No," answered Zhou. "The texts had been written in the 14th or 15th century by a foreigner of Central Asia."

The second part, or *Dastan,* is made of stories that one tells, stories that have no link between them. The scenes occur at the hairdresser, at a meal, at the market. The third category, *Maxirep* (pronounce Meshrep), consists of song and dance. It is presented during official festivals as well as family festivities. *Maxirep* follows the calendar: it has bonds with work, climate, harvest, society, and the rural life especially. *Maxirep* is even the name of an activity: there is a *maxirep* for a wedding, one for a friend's visit, and one for the New Year's Day, and so on. *Maxirep* reveals the Uyghurs' hearts: it expresses feelings, interpersonal relationships, way of solving problems, and moral education.

The general repetition starts immediately after this "lesson." To pass from folk art to professional art is far from easy. It is however the challenge that Zhou Ji has won. Even the composition of the program for this show is proof of it: the three categories of Muqam will take the stage in turn.

For instance, at the very beginning of *Qiongnagemam*, the music of only one wind instrument can be heard; little by little, the drums are added; then a single dancer, followed by two; women join, then three children. Rhythm intensifies, marked by dance and percussion mainly. In *Dastan*, there is a question between two men coveting the same woman, while *Maxirep* shows, among the peasants who dance in their fields, a camel and a goose

"inhabited" by dancers. In addition, some Tajik and Kirgiz artists take part in the huge event called "Silk Road 2007."

Born in Jiangsu, Zhou Ji arrived in Xinjiang at the age of 17. In addition to studying the Uyghur language, he who already had a training in music started to study *rewap*, a typical Uyghur instrument. I asked Zhou to repeat this name several times so that I could reproduce the phonetic pronunciation. What I heard, in fact, was something between *rewap* and *ravop*.

Today, the Muqam specialist is known in the whole country and he has won the appreciation of the Xinjiang government. He is deputy director, vice-president, professor, lecturer, representative, invited researcher, doctoral adviser, etc., in various high-level institutions and associations of Chinese traditional music, folk music, ethnic music, and Xinjiang music in the whole territory of China, including Hong Kong. Needless to say Zhou Ji often travels back and forth between Xinjiang and the national capital.

The master has published 12 works and three others are under preparation; he has written articles about music and dance of the country's western region and also songs. Zhou has mastered the Uyghur language. He has been asked more than once to translate Muqam texts into Chinese, but he refused, saying that "music and language

are inseparable forms and an untranslatable whole."

Zhou has won personal prizes, but if a reward includes Muqam, he feels that his efforts are recognized and is as proud of it. The most recent of these recognitions is a photograph of two 78-year-old Muqam interpreters – handsome old men still full of vigor, who sing, dance, and play instruments – being embraced by Prime Minister Wen Jiabao on June 9, 2007. While proudly showing the large picture to the imaginary public during the repetition, Zhou said that it was a symbol of the importance that the state attaches to the protection of Muqam

– an intangible inheritance of humanity, as recognized by the United Nations Educational, Scientific, and Cultural Organization (UNESCO) in 2005.

His soul "carried by Uyghurs," Zhou has completely integrated into the Uyghur culture. He even ended up resembling the men of this ethnic group and, like most of them, wears the beard. "If not for my southern accent, one would confuse me with them," he said with a certain pride. From 1987, Zhou dedicated two years to listening Muqam "until my ears felt like bursting," remembered the greatest specialist, in order to transcribe the scores correctly. And this was how he came to understand the beauty of Muqam.

That UNESCO placed Muqam on its list of treasures which constitute the heritage of humanity does not release Zhou Ji of his responsibility. "On the contrary, it increases the pressure," he acknowledged. Moreover, he received only 25,000 yuan from the state to defray his research expenses. I asked whether this allowance was annual. He smiled: "No, once, forever!" The lack of funds does not allow him to look further into his research. Fortunately, some friends, as impassioned as he is for Muqam, support him with their own money and services: photographs, recording, etc. In addition, Xinjiang opened about 15 centres for safeguarding Muqam. In Turpan, the local government pays the Muqam "professionals"

400 yuan a month so they can teach the art and put on shows. Dancers, singers and musicians – a hundred people of which the youngest is six years old – are for the majority farmers who take part according to their availability.

What makes Muqam altogether exclusive and difficult is that a large part is written in an archaic language that is no longer spoken. The singers memorize texts that they don't understand. More, the sections are long – from 10 minutes to an hour – and the content is complex; memorizing it is not a vacation. No singer can remember a complete work; each one can sing only three, four, or five parts at most.

What worried Zhou Ji particularly is that the researchers are currently all Han. He wished that his efforts will produce enthusiastic and qualified amateurs who will continue on his footsteps.

When Zhou studied the flute in Shanghai where he attended high school, his teacher gave him a piece to interpret that the student found very beautiful. But he didn't know that it was precisely an extract of Muqam. Once in Xinjiang, the young Zhou attended the troop of songs and dances of Xinjiang, and in 1961, this troop went to Beijing to give a special representation titled *Following Mao Zedong Step by Step*. Then, in 1964, when he was growing corn with the Uyghur peasants, he heard them singing popular love songs. In the traditional Chinese society, one did not speak of love. Zhou thought that Uyghurs were more open and simple than the Han. All of that prepared him for his future mission, while instilling in him a passion for Muqam and the Uyghur culture that feeds it.

Uyghurs had to work extremely hard to transform the desert into nourishing earth. Overcoming misery and solitude by singing together strengthened them. Muqam is rooted in the hearts of the Uyghurs who love it and respect it.

The repetition was over and a resumption was going to start. Since Zhou Ji's task was not finished he could not give me more time but cordially invited me to go to his place the following day to talk some more. Unfortunately, I had to decline the invitation: a plane was waiting for me; I was leaving for northern Xinjiang.

May the music explode in the peoples' hearts! This is Zhou Ji's wish.

THE HIDE AND SOUL OF A WILD HORSE

Zhang Hefan, Han

"It has been raining for eight hours. The ground is like a sponge and the horses are filthy," warned Zhang Hefan over the phone. From Urumqi, one can reach the Wild Horse Research and Reproduction Centre of Jimsar, in Changji Hui Autonomous Prefecture, in an hour and a half. The young woman was waiting for me with the Centre's deputy director, Ma Dan, 39, a Kazak, as was most of the staff.

Zhang Hefan is 33. With her small frame, she looks like a little girl. She was born in Xinjiang Tacheng (Qoqen) to a mother from Henan Province and a father from Jiangsu, who met in Xinjiang in the 1960s. She is the second of four children, two girls and two boys, all born within five years. Her parents could not afford advanced education for all of the children. In addition,

her father – from the age of 40 – suffered from an illness and could not work. Only Hefan and her youngest brother attended university. Now, her older sister has established herself in their mother's province where she owns a hair salon, and her two brothers are a driver and a policeman.

Zhang chose to become a veterinarian because, when she was at the Xinjiang University of Agriculture, students were encouraged to choose a discipline "that would benefit Xinjiang." Also, Zhang Hefan had always loved animals and had raised dogs and cats as a child.

Once she graduated in July 1995, the 21-year-old arrived at the Wild Horse Research and Reproduction

Centre, 140 km from Urumqi, where her family was then living. After an arduous journey just to get there, she noticed upon arrival that the Centre did not have electricity, and that there was no telephone, no television, no store in the immediate vicinity, and no fresh fruits and vegetables to be had in close proximity. All around her was the vast gobi desert. All that confronted her was an enormous horseshed and small earthen houses for the 15-member staff, of whom there was only one woman: Zhang. Faced with these rudimentary life and work conditions and without any communication with the outside world, she could only cry. Often, she was tempted to quit, she disclosed, but every time she prepared her letter of resignation, one of her "friends" needed her, such as a sick horse or a horse that had problems delivering a foal. She didn't have the heart to abandon them.

The Centre deals with preservation and reproduction of the Prjevalski (also Przewalski) horse. This name came from a Russian colonel who, in 1878, believed he had discovered this breed of horse although it had already occupied Hans Schiltberger's memories who, in 1427, lived in the Tianshan Mountains (after being a prisoner of the Turks who traded him for a Mongol prince) where he had an opportunity to carefully study the wild horses and meticulously write down his observations. The *Equus caballus prejwalski* is also called a Kertag horse, Mongol

Tarpan, Taki (from Mongolian "Takh") or, simply, Asia wild horse. In the Lascaux Grottoes of France, and on the Altamira rock paintings in Spain, the existence of this horse was evident, and one can see how old this race is, protected intuitively in a sense by its natural hostility towards intruders, thus enabling its preservation. It was said that 60 million years ago, the wild horse was about as small as today's fox. Around the end of 20th century, the Prjevalski horse had been wiped out from the Asian grasslands by a "civilization" that ignored the rules of nature and science. When the Jimsar Centre opened in 1986, it imported 11 horses from England and East Germany to establish its livestock and, later, others from the United States and Russia – two countries where most of them can be found today. Zhang estimates their global number at 1,400, a little fewer than the number of pandas – 1,700. Both species are under the highest level of state protection.

Breeding wild horses is easy, said Zhang Hefan, but the first birth is often risky. "The survival rate is 98 percent in China, while abroad it is around 25 percent." Although I think I misunderstood her, Zhang confirmed that such a miracle is possible because the horse is in its original and natural environment.

Then comes the privileged moment: seeing the horses on terra firma. I observed the 49 males and notice a great resemblance to the wild donkey, with a stocky body, dun coat, short and dark mane, elongated head, large muzzle, thick neck, and powerful legs. Zhang agreed with my observations while constantly reminding me to stay in front of the horse. Even when the horse itself moved about, I had to stay in its line of vision. Otherwise it would immediately balk. Zhang had to do the same as I, even though she was their "friend."

A clan includes one stallion and five to 12 mares. When a mare becomes pregnant, it seeks a quiet place to give birth and then returns to the herd with its foal, which grows quickly. Moreover, the baby can stand 20 minutes after its birth, and, an hour later, is already solid on its legs. A female gives birth once a year after a one-year

gestation. The birthing period is thus concentrated between April and July.

If a man or another male horse comes near one of the females, the stallion will lead the intruder away from the herd and the opponents will fight in a standing position, with their front hooves, or by balking and biting. However, if a human or a male horse comes too close to a foal, the mother is the one that will protect its offspring. I noticed scars – even large and deep ones – and holes in the horses' hides. "Those are battle wounds," Zhang explained. A horse may break a leg in a fight and even lose its life. When the colt or the filly reaches about two years of age, the father chases them from the clan and literally kicks them out if they don't obey at first. They are considered adults and have to establish a new family elsewhere. The mother doesn't interfere, as nature prevails.

The Prjevalski horse is considered stubborn and nimble with quick reflexes. It can also run 60 km per hour and could be domesticated for horseback riding, but taming the wild horse is exactly what the Centre wants to avoid.

Jimsar is located northeast of Urumqi. Further in the same direction, one finds an immense rough terrain that will become the Karamaili-protected natural reserve with 16,000 sq km. It is at Karamaili that the Centre, aiming

to cultivate the wild horses, frees the animals when they are ready. Six years ago, the Centre began sending horses back to their natural habitat, but until then they are not completely independent. The potential danger for them happens when, instead of feeding themselves from the grassland, they approach domestic herds and eat their food. There is also the danger that they will mate with domestic animals, which interferes with the breed's strain. That is why they have to be constantly monitored. Their current number allows scientists not to consider them as a potentially extinct species, unless they are left to their own devices. Horses wear an ID neck band. Cooperation with the United States and the Cologne Centre of Germany remains high with regard to equipment and technical support. Cologne gave five horses to Jimsar, two of which have already been freed. The Centre also gave 15 horses to Shanghai in 1995, two to Altay, and 15 to the Urumqi Zoo in 2004 and 2005, respectively.

Zhang Hefan wrote a book excerpting some pages of her diary and some love stories of the horses. I read a deeply moving page and was eager to hear her talk about life at the Centre. Zhang, in subtly poetic comparisons, had stressed the loneliness of the horses, which also mirrored her emotional state. The perfect calm, the silence of the place, struck me as soon as I arrived. No one was around: the staff was not numerous and the activity field was expansive. No booming radio or TV – only an occasional whinny.

Zhang Hefan's work at the Centre constitutes a remarkable contribution. Zhang had reorganized and compiled the collateral genealogy of the horses, which is the only way to avoid inbreeding. Mating is not random at the Centre; experts choose mares for each stallion according to their genealogy. On the occasion that a male rejects a female, the female is replaced. Due to Zhang's diligent work, for 294 births the inbreeding is below 0.2 percent and annual reproduction exceeds 21 percent.

Zhang has never been wounded by a horse but some of her colleagues have. The most dangerous moment is when one needs to lasso a horse, such as when it requires treatment.

In front of the Centre is a large expanse of bright flowers, of which Deputy Director Ma Dan was very proud: "We have not changed the soil; it is the local earth that produced all this!" In the uncultivated area, red willow (*hongliu*) bloomed freely. This plant requires little water and is thus suitable for desert conditions. The Centre's ground is huge and unexploited up to now. Administration could save much of its expenses by growing forage on its 600 hectares.

If the desert is Zhang Hefan's homeland, the horses are her children. She named her favourite ones "Prince,"

"Princess," "Snow Lotus," "Commander-in-Chief," and "Xiu Xiu." Zhang claimed: "I already took the horses' skin color, I want to have their soul." In the 12 years that Zhang has spent at the Centre, conditions have improved greatly. Two years ago, the Centre was relocated to a new building. New, comfortable apartments have been allocated to the staff that now numbers 40. In addition, more and more visitors come.

However, among the specialists, Zhang is still the only woman. Certainly she would like to marry, but will she be able to? There are no bachelors among her male colleagues who live at the Centre, and their wives and children live in town. A few years ago, the schedule was modified and 18 days of work are now followed by 12 days off, allowing a worker a chance to go home to see his family. Personnel is needed constantly. Horses must be fed four times a day, the last feeding being at midnight. In the winter, carrots and cereal gruel are added to the hay diet for more substance. Before, employees had holidays for Spring Festival (Chinese New Year) and once again during the year, but they didn't always have time to enjoy their vacation.

According to Zhang, she doesn't feel stressed and finds her work very pleasant and not overwhelming, with no deadlines. Her task consists of vaccinating the animals, treating the sick, and helping to deliver foals. She no longer feels lonely as she did before and claims she is happy.

She would like to travel when she is off, but said that her salary – 400 yuan at the beginning, more than 1,000 now (plus a three-month allowance at year end) – won't accommodate that. On the other hand, she enjoys free housing, medical insurance, and a pension plan. When she goes back to Urumqi, she stays at home cleaning, reading, and writing. She has published a book of 75 poems about horses.

She has little contact with former classmates, and when I asked if she had friends, she answered that her colleagues were her friends. I explained that the word "friend" has a different meaning in Western culture, and concluded, "So you have no friends." I can't help but think that her horses, with which she created unseverable ties, are her friends, in fact.... She no longer thinks about leaving the Centre; her heart has taken root there.

In her book *Wild Horse – Return to Karamaili*, an unexpected success – the author said that she wanted only one thing: that more people become interested in protecting and saving wild horses. No wonder she calls herself "Yema Hefan" (Wild Horse Hefan).

I offered Zhang the chance to use the car that was slated to take me back to Urumqi. Her 12-day leave began that day. On the road, we continued to chat. "The night before graduation," she recounted, "I had a dream: a heavenly horse rushed right up to me. It was superb, vital, and elegant. I didn't know yet that I had been assigned to the Xinjiang Wild Horse Centre. This has been a recurring dream throughout the years."

Then she told me the story of Snow Lotus – the filly that before had pushed me against the fence in a burst of energy. She was only 21 days old when her mother died from a heat wave in the region. The ground temperature had reached 65 degrees Celsius. This news rapidly spread around Xinjiang, and pupils from the whole region "adopted" the orphan by giving one yuan each for a total amount of 14,000 yuan. They also chose her name by voting.

I asked Zhang to personally tell me a moving story that I had read in an article she wrote: the story of Stallion No. 34, whose loneliness was pitiful in front of the iron gate, despite his fierce and stoic appearance. "To return to wild life might be the ultimate aspiration of any wild horse," wrote Zhang. "Freedom literally: vertical and horizontal!"

In October 2007, Zhang Hefan's Wild Horse – Return to Karamaili *has been awarded the "Five Cultural Works Prize" (book, film, teleseries, drama, song) by the Communist Youth League of China, her sixth award in the last two years for outstanding contribution to the Xinjiang culture.*

BOWS AND ARROWS

Yilari·Chunguang, Xibe

After a 90-minute flight from Urumqi, we landed at the Yining (Gulja) Airport in Ili Kazak Autonomous Prefecture – a green island – where 46 ethnic groups live. I was accompanied to Ili (or Seman) Hotel – headquarters of the Russian Consulate before Liberation, that later became the powerful Nikolai Petrovsky's residence – and we immediately set off for Qapqal ("Chabucha'er" in Chinese) Xibe Autonomous County, 17 km further southwest. The temperature of 27°C and a sunny blue sky were auspicious signs to me.

There we arrived at Yi Chunguang's place. He shortened his original name, Yilari·Chunguang. Chunguang means "spring light." The house kitten welcomed me along with its master and immediately became very friendly.

Yi Chunguang was the first Xibe (also Xibo) I met. Originally from Dongbei (a name designating the three northeast provinces of the country), they number 120,000 in Liaoning, but Yi said that "there," Xibe don't speak their national language anymore. In Xinjiang, they total fewer, about 33,000, two-thirds being in Qapqal, but their culture still flourishes. Census surveys show that there are Xibe in all the Chinese provinces, even though there are only 18 in Hainan and two in Tibet.

Their written language is derived from Manchu and comprises 108 letters. In fact, to decode the ancient writings found in the Beijing Imperial Palace, six old Xibe were consulted, as they were the only ones who could still interpret Manchu. Few Xibe write in their language today. They have for the most part adopted Chinese, though the Xibe language is still spoken at home. "We Xibe mostly practice Shamanism," Yi explained. "Some are Buddhist. There is no ban on marrying outside the ethnic group and many do. My niece's husband is Han, my three daughters-in-law are Han. So, we end up adopting the Han language, customs, and celebrations, while preserving our own, such as the Bow Festival, on the 18th day of the fourth month," he added.

How and why did the Xibe people arrive in Xinjiang? "Xibe is a people of archers. In 1764, Emperor Qianlong of the Qing Dynasty sent 3,000 to 4,000 Xibe from Shenyang, the capital of Liaoning Province, to defend the northwest borders." Why the Xibe? "Because our ancestors were known for their archery skills. The emperor armed them, writing down the number of arrows for each one – six or eight for soldiers and up to

12 to 20 for officers. When they arrived in Xinjiang, they totalled 4,500." Why such a rise in number? I think they had probably recruited forces along the way, but my interlocutor smiled. "Children were born during the 16-month voyage!" adding, "It was quick, as usually two years were needed to travel the distance."

The route was estimated to be 6,000 km until 2006, when a Chinese person covered it by motorcycle to calculate the exact length, which is now known to be 7,800 km. Part of the route is now in the Mongolia territory. The Xibe moved around on foot or oxen carts. Only the leaders of the group rode a horse, even when fighting. "The Qing Dynasty emperors also sent the Xibe to chase the Burmese from Yunnan, to suppress a rebellion in Sichuan, and to resist the Russian Tsarist invasion. Archery has a history of 30,000 years in the world. For our Xibe ancestors, to bear a scar from an arrow was a decoration and to die from an arrow, an honor.

"We are all descended from these archers," continued Yi Chunguang. "The emperor had told them that in 60 years, they could go back home, but when the deadline came, Qianlong had died and the Xibe had formed roots in Xinjiang."

I observed the man while he talked, punctuating his sentences with short but resounding laughter, and I

thought he resembled Ewenki and the Oroqen people. "In fact," he replied, "we northeast people share common features, and also with the Japanese and the Koreans."

As his wife, Jiao Yuxiang, who is seriously diabetic, started to lose her sight at the age of 50 following an incorrect diagnosis 10 years earlier (which cost 60,000 yuan), Yi decided to retire before term, in 1998, to take care of her. Both are now 60. "She is better than many other sick people whose condition is not as bad, because she practices *qigong* (a technique for vital energy circulation in the body) regularly." In the evenings, Yi likes to sit in the garden and play the accordion for his wife. His cooking skills are not bad, and he even likes to do house chores. When his three sons, their wives, and four children come from Urumqi to spend holidays at home, he takes care of everything. Yi gets a retirement pension of 1,400 yuan a month, which is enough, he said. He could have had more if he had worked at only one place, but he had five jobs during his working life, including farm worker, carpenter, road builder, school attendant. From 1994 to 1996, he conducted business with foreign countries. "Pakistan, Kazakhstan, Tajikistan.... I went to all these countries," explained Yi, who is fluent in six languages.

One day, while visiting an antiques market in Beijing, he saw a long arrow that had a price tag of 4,800 yuan.

"It was very ugly," specified Yi. "I thought that our own Xibe arrows were made much better and that I could certainly make some. Why not, as I made all my furniture?" he added, laughingly. "I can design, engrave, varnish. There is probably a market for my bows and arrows, I thought. So, I went back home and started to study models from the collection of bows and arrows of the Xibe who arrived in 1764, and I drew sketches. Then, I started to make some. Nine years now! I can get cow hide here for the quivers, but I also buy some from Shandong, Mongolia and elsewhere to compare quality. What is difficult to find is sheep intestines for the string. There are also ox tendons. The bow is made from a variety of wood and fibreglass, and also ram horn." Yi described how to make a quality bow, the invisible seams of the parts, the position of the arrow at the right or left of the bow, and how the fingers bend the bow according to the Xibe technique or the Western technique. Listening to Yi, I learned a great deal again.

Yi's house has become a tourist spot, as indicated by a brass plaque at the yard's entrance. Media are interested in Yi's work, and the TV anchor Jiao Jianchang, also a Xibe, is filming Xibe culture in the region.

I asked Yi Chunguang whether he intended to gather the fruits of his research in a book. "It has been done!" he said, underscoring his answer with

laughter. "Here it is. I'm not educated enough to write a book by myself. I found someone. I provided all the data and paid the expense, and it has become a cooperative effort."

Today, Yi has his own trademark and a modest workshop. He has hired four women and three men. He draws the models, and the workers cut and assemble the leather. He sews the quivers and decorates them with

animals such as the Xibe totem – *Ruishou* (literally "auspicious animal"), a mythical figure – or a rabbit or ox. Before this book is published, the workshop will have expanded.

Yi has three grandsons and one granddaughter. When a boy is born, a little arrow is suspended to a red thread in front of the house. The third day after birth, his parents or grandparents shoot an arrow in each of the cardinal directions, praying for the child to be brave and to have an indomitable spirit.

At four or five, the child receives a bow and arrows appropriate for his age and he starts preliminary training. But at 16, the training turns rigorous and the boy must learn how to shoot arrows from a running horse and participate in all the folkloric festivals and competitions. At the age of 18, he must take an exam that involves shooting arrows from a running horse and also enrol as a

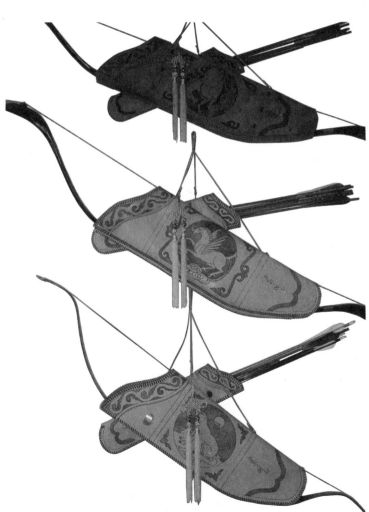

soldier who is able to defend the territory. The Xibe have maintained this tradition; does it mean that they are warriors?

"No," answered Yi. "Our ancestors were nomads who lived by hunting. This is what mastering the shooting of arrows serves to accomplish." As they had become, by that fact, very skilful archers, they have been used in defending the country.

The Xibe have typical dishes such as *Jiazgen*, composed of braised beef, potatoes, carrots, "*piaz*" (onions) and long, dry beans like the ones that the ancestors had brought over from Liaoning. They also have a thick pancake called *fa'erv*. The darker side, coloured by baking, represents the sky and the white side, the earth. The eating custom is to hold the *fa'erv* with the "sky" side up and fill it with cucumbers, peppers, and eggplant, which will then be enclosed in the fold, or to use the chopsticks to fill the *fa'erv*, always with the "earth" part inside.

This century is promising for Yi Chunguang: in addition to obtaining a patent for his bows and arrows, he won the silver medal in the category of "excellent tourist goods" and the second prize in a shooting competition in which 160 countries participated.

HUMAN WARMTH
AS A BONUS

Ili people can barely tolerate the day's temperature of 32 degrees. Coming from Beijing where the humidity exacerbates the heaviness of the heat, I felt comfortable on this "forced holiday." I had only one interview to conduct in Ili, but the local Information Office had been so thoughtfully accommodating to me that I could not respond with ingratitude. So, the time that I had planned to dedicate to work became an opportunity for a wonderful exploration of the region.

The Ili Kazak Autonomous Prefecture borders Russia, Mongolia, and Kazakhstan. An interesting spot for tourists is the Korgas ("Huo'erguosi" in Chinese) International Trade Port, in the west, from where Kazakhstan's mountains can be seen. A bilateral commercial zone is under construction and should open in

2009. On the Chinese side, 3.43 sq km will be dedicated to it, and 1.2 sq km on the Kazak side.

Next, we visited Huiyuan, 30 km from Yining, the Ili Jiangjunfu or the Ili Military High Command, where the regional administrative centre was in 1757, before the establishment of Xinjiang Province in 1884, with Urumqi as its capital. The vast complex included a complete *siheyuan* as one can see in Beijing, and a large museum where I had a chance to hear a skilful guide summarize the local history and tell the moving story of the life, exile, and death of Lin Zexu, a character that has always deeply impressed me.

After lunch – taken here at 14:00 – I was asked, "Do you like landscapes?" I could not refuse the invitation because, in Xinjiang, they are wonderfully gorgeous and varied.

And then we were on our way to Sayram Lake in Bortala Mongol Autonomous Prefecture, a two hours' drive headed northeast of Korgas. Along the road, wonderful panoramas revealed themselves, one after the other. Evergreen trees, each close to the other, upright in the sky. The tallest were about the height of a three-story building. Here was a completely vertical waterfall; there, a mountain slope covered with mulberry trees. I was intrigued by the construction of a highway between Guozigou (the Apple Pass) and Sayram Lake, an elevated

highway that will reach 210 m at its higher point. And there was so much cement! Was that absolutely necessary? The following day, I was informed that the present road was extremely dangerous; with frequent floods and heavy snowfall, it becomes impassable or fatally slippery. The height of the new road will solve these two major problems.

Finally came Sayram Lake, 2,071 m above sea level. There, the water reflected the azure of the sky, and the snow-capped mountains compose the background. Facing the lake, the natural landscape off Sayram Lake can be enjoyed. But, facing the bank, a permanent fair that attracts tourists is in view: camel rides and rides on carts pulled by goats, souvenir photos, fresh beverages, and local products. Unfortunately, I noticed that the visitors had little respect for the environment.

All around on the mountain slopes, the establishment of tourism and *Dujiacun* (holiday villages) made for brisk business. Vacationers like to experience living in a Mongolian tent, to walk among the sheep, or to ride a Kazak horse.

On our way back, we followed a little truck carrying a mosque "crown" made of three balls and a moon crescent. I told my companions that I had not seen many mosques up to now. Xinjiang has 23,753, as more than 60 percent of the population practice Islam. In Ili Prefecture alone, there are 1,200 mosques, at least one in

each of the 700 villages, I was told. There are more where
the Hui people are densely concentrated. Could they be
more religious than the Uyghur, Kazak, and other

Muslim people? I had to enquire about this ....

At the farewell dinner, which I hoped was only a temporary goodbye, representatives of the local

(Front) On both sides of the author, a Buyei and a Mongol.
(Back) A Russian, two Han, and a Uyghur.

government and of information organisations honored me with their presence. The two highest posts are held by women, one Buyei, one Mongol. I suddenly realized that the seven guests, including myself, were from six nations, a typical image of colorful Xinjiang and of Ili, where 46 ethnic groups live.

WE ARE COMPEERS

Bahetiehan·Salimbahe, Kazak

Since I have been living in China, every time I travel in the country, I pay special attention to education. I am probably influenced by a 30-year teaching career. This is what I did in June 2005 when visiting Xinjiang. I had been impressed, then, not only by the excellent condition of the Woyimoke school in Burqin County (Altay Prefecture), but by the warm welcome reserved for us. It was a business trip and it was a Sunday. Pupils had been asked to go to school on their normal day off in return for a Monday off. Children offered us a musical and dance performance in the schoolyard before quietly returning to their classrooms. They were unfazed by our camera flashes and our circulating between their rows of tables. Afterward, the school headmaster and all of the teachers prepared a superb dinner that ended in

dancing and laughter. We departed with refrains of "next time," "you will come back," etc., but at the bottom of my heart, I thought I would never see these people again and this obscure land in the far north of Xinjiang. However, the interviews needed for writing the present book offered me a new opportunity, and I asked to interview a young male teacher in whom I had found a sentient being, Pazli·Hablhahe, during my former visit. But I was told that Pazli had left. Disappointed but not defeated, I requested to interview the school headmaster instead.

Immediately after landing – a 50-minute flight between Ili and Altay – I was accompanied to Burqin, which was a 90-minute car ride. There, another car waited, in which the headmaster, Bahetiehan·Salimbahe, and the chief of the Burqin Information Bureau, Bahetibek·Axmhan, were sitting. They led us to the

Moaibas Village school. Bahetibek served as an interpreter, translating from the Kazak language to Chinese. On the narrow earth road full of stones, the cars whipped up dust. I thought, 'nothing has changed from two years ago,' and I asked myself if there would be as many mosquitoes. Yes, mosquitoes were present and were not at all shy! They didn't miss their great opportunity to fill up with the fresh blood that had come from afar.

The headmaster removed the tiny lock on the wooden door, and we entered his office. Not a soul could be seen in and around the school; summer holidays were in full mode. A female teacher who could speak Chinese had been invited to come again to meet me. Wasina·Taiman had taught me a Kazak dance two years ago, and I had given my silk scarf to her as a gift. She had not forgotten

me and it was heart-warming to see this.

Bahetiehan, 48, took the interview very seriously. Sitting at his desk, he thoughtfully answered my questions while asking questions of his own and at the same time took notes in Kazak. The headmaster confirmed to me that the rate of compulsory education – nine years – is always 100 percent, and that this occurred not only in his township but everywhere in Xinjiang. Schooling and textbooks are free; children don't have to pay any tuition. As indicated by a brass plate above the door, the Woyimoke school was opened under the auspices of Project Hope, a social welfare education program under the China Youth Development Foundation.

As evidenced by the Kazak cemetery, Burqin County is populated by Kazaks, who were nomads earlier. The government encouraged 3,415 families to change their way of life. To this end, they distributed land to cultivate corn and livestock food. The children of nomadic families used to follow their parents with the herds and so could not receive an education. Now, they attend school. In fact, four out of five families remain at home while the fifth takes all the livestock to the mountains in summer. When winter comes, the herdsmen return with the animals and station them close to the house. The double harvest of forage suffices for them all, while before, with harsh winters and abundant snow, the animals would

have died of hunger. The rate of settlement was around 86 percent in 2005. Another miracle hard to imagine consists in these thousands of hectares that used to be expanses of *gobi* (stone). Humans have appropriated land from the desert.

Schools can be found everywhere now and, generally, schools must be built closely enough so that the children do not have to walk more than 12 km a day. The average is presently five km in each direction; it is the case for all the Woyimoke students, except for 15, who walk or cycle to school. Needless to say, these children lunch at school, rather than making a return trip home for that meal.

Woyimoke had 248 pupils in 2005 and now has 232; all of them are Kazak. There are a few more girls than boys. From 21 teachers previously, they now have 20 for 10 classes, including two pre-school classes. I asked the third grade teacher, Pazli·Hablhahe, who had 22 students, what his main problem was. He answered, "Material difficulty, as our school has no electricity; pedagogical difficulty, as teaching the Chinese language to children who never hear this language except at school is not easy; and logistical difficulty, as children have to walk far and are tired." In the next class of the second grade, there were 37 students, three per bench, and only one teacher for all the subjects. I also noticed that teachers spoke Chinese with a very strong accent. Most knew enough Chinese to pass a written exam, but they could not communicate verbally. This aspect of the situation has not changed, I noted.

Pazli was gone, but for other reasons than those I thought. He now teaches politics in a high school of Burqin where his family lives, which makes his life easier. A Woyimoke school headmaster earns 2,500 yuan a month and teachers earn between 1,200 and 2,500, including bonuses, according to their competence and seniority. They benefit from a medical insurance and a pension fund.

During the summer holidays, children have homework to do at home and they go back to the school monthly to meet their teachers and to hand in what they have completed.

What improvements has the school accomplished in two years? The headmaster was proud to answer. First,

teaching by computer. A portable television with a giant screen can be moved from class to class. The central government provided the school with two computers, which also serve for administration purposes. I saw them beside a printer, a photocopier, and a typewriter – the type that can be seen in museums. Second, children begin learning Chinese in the first grade. Chinese is taught by four Kazak teachers who are all graduates from Urumqi or Changji advanced learning establishments and who have one to four years' experience. Third, the teachers' apartments and surrounding grounds have improved. Fourth, all teachers go to Urumqi or elsewhere in turn for improvement courses. These classes are partly subsidized by the school and partly by the Burqin Education Bureau.

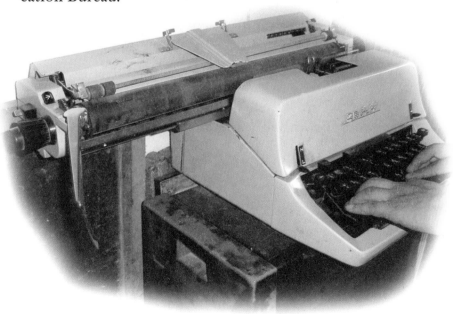

All the Moaibas children attend local school. In middle school, they go to a boarding school. Only food fees are imposed on the families. The best students, about 15 percent of them, are chosen to continue their studies in a high school under Shihezi University or in special Kazak classes elsewhere in the country.

The school library is composed of four shelves of books in Chinese and in Kazak, as offered by the China Youth Development Foundation.

We leafed through French and English editions of magazines that had published my articles about Xinjiang. Bahetiehan could "read" the images only. Then he asked me questions about my family, and I, about his. I found out that he has three sons. The eldest is a driver, the second one just graduated from high school, and the youngest graduated from middle school.

Bahetiehan's wife is 46 years old. She also is a teacher at Woyimoke. That evening, she joined us for a dinner which was enlivened with music, and, obviously, I could not avoid looking silly as I tried to follow her steps in a Kazak dance.

CAPS THAT FLY

Jina, Russian

It is in the "tourist Burqin" that is under construction where the talkative, loudly laughing, and sturdy 76-year-old woman lives. Far from being an advantage, living in her house, which is made of a row of adobe rooms, brings her stress. "Every day I am told that I have to move, that they will demolish it. I don't know when but for certain I will have to leave," said Jina. As she owns an apartment in town, she will not be homeless, but what is presently her little shop and her stockroom will disappear. "I want to be compensated. They should give me a place somewhere, or a garage," she claimed rightly. That will surely be done, but the uncertainty darkens her horizon.

Jina was born in Russia and she doesn't know exactly where. Her parents came to China when she was six years old. "They settled at Kaba ("Habahe" in Chinese), an hour from here by road. They said they left the country because of war. They were not alone," she added. "Many Russians came to live in Xinjiang at that time." In 1956, Xinjiang Russians moved again, mostly to Australia. "They all left. I remained alone. My elder brother went to Canada," she recounted, showing me an envelope bearing a Vancouver (a city in British Columbia, Canada) return address. "I was pregnant with my third child. My brother had no children and I wanted to give my daughter for him to raise, but he didn't wait around for her to be born," continued Jina in a disappointed tone. After her sister-in-law died in Canada, she never heard from her brother. "She was the one who wrote. Now, my brother

is lost to me."

Jina grew up in Xinjiang where she attended school for one or two years. However, she learned to write Russian by herself and enough Chinese to read a book or the newspapers. "I also speak Kazak, and I can manage in Uyghur," she added laughingly.

She met her husband at the age of 17. "He used to pull on my long braids, and I rapped his hands. He was a handsome man, you know!"

Jina was a worker in a metal equipment factory. "The boss was a Kazak, and his assistant was a Han. I often acted as an interpreter for them." Then, she retired. "My two sons have two sons each, and my daughter is a mother of two girls. Four of my grandchildren graduated from university. Many children mean much money. To each of my six grandchildren I give 100 yuan monthly." That is why Jina decided in 1982 to start making *kvas*, a Russian word for beer. Her husband used to work with her until he died from asthma in 2000. "At that moment, there was no *kvas* in the region. Nobody had ever tasted it. Here, under this roof which supported the hops, there was a long communal table and people came to drink in the evening." Customers were all Kazak in the beginning; then, more and more Han people came. "The Kazak like the bitter taste of hops in the *kvas*, while the Han prefer the sweet taste of the honey." The number of foreigners will surely increase with the burgeoning tourism in Burqin, which is a crossroad of communications in Altay Prefecture. "Foreign tourists come from Europe and Japan, but I mostly serve local tourists, and many of them are Russian."

A decade ago, a night market opened in a neighbouring street. This is where Jina and her daughter-in-law, Yelia, go every day around 19:00, each pedalling a tricycle loaded with bottles. Till midnight or sometimes till 2:00, they serve *kvas* and fresh yogurt made that day. "Before, a bottle of beer cost 0.3 yuan; now, it costs 2 yuan. You can only have the empty bottle for 0.3 yuan now!" Jina makes more than 100 bottles a day. "Some

bottles may remain, sometimes not. Other people have started to make *kvas* too, but customers seem to prefer mine. They say that the others '*Mei you eluosi lao taitai de weidao*' – 'don't have the old Russian lady's taste.'" *Eluosi lao taitai* is also Jina's trademark. She handcrafts her own brand of tags and sticks them, one by one, on the bottles. She doesn't plan to industrialize her production or to register her brand name. "This beer must be drunk fresh; after two or three days, the taste fades. Moreover, fermentation makes the caps jump. You see, these little caps just have to jump in the air and don't hurt anyone. I tried to use big black caps I had bought and to make others by myself using old tires, but

customers put them in their pockets!" At the night market, hearing the joyous explosion of a cap, the customers rush on "that" bottle, because they know the sound signals that the bottle is at its best. So, Jina pursues her enterprise at her own pace, with her daughter-in-law and a student who helps her during the holidays. She earns enough, as her investment was practically nothing. The water comes from the well in the courtyard and the hops come from the mountains; in addition to sugar or honey (according to the season), only time and labor are required. The process is simple and no special equipment is required. Five months out of the year, the climate doesn't allow the opening of the night market, which provides a rest for "the old Russian lady."

When she was young, Jina liked to swim in the Ertix. The whole family used to go, including their dog! Every year, Russians celebrate Orthodox Easter on the Ertix's bank with a huge picnic where families take their best homemade dish. Following the meal, they sing and dance to the accompaniment of an accordion and other musical instruments, and exchange hand-painted eggs. Several Russian have married Han, enlarging the ethnic family. Some Han who are not linked to the Russians take part in these celebrations, too. "There is also a Jewish person who comes and he sings very well," said Jina. Some people spend two days on the bank.

THE DOOR OF DESTINY

Jiang'er·Rehati, Kazak

J iang'er·Rehati lives in northeast Xinjiang, at Fuhai (Burultokay) in Altay Prefecture. I arrived at her place from Burqin on a Sunday morning; she expected me at the entrance of the modest courtyard to her nice, large, and comfortable house. As in all the Kazak houses I visited, I noticed the presence of lovely carpets in each room. Jiang'er stopped me from taking off my shoes. In fact, she had taken the precaution of rolling up the living room carpet. Underneath, white ceramic tiles looked easy to clean.

Born in Manas, Changji Hui Autonomous Prefecture, Jiang'er is the eldest of four children. She has a sister and two brothers, of whom one is a professor, and the other two, office cadres. When Jiang'er was a child, her family came to live in Fuhai, and in 1986 returned to Manas.

She remained.

Jiang'er looked tired, and for good reason. Two hours earlier, she had just returned from a four-day meeting in Urumqi. It was a preparatory meeting for the 17th National Congress of the Communist Party in October. Jiang'er was recently elected to participate in it, and her term will last five years. As soon as she passed through the door of her home, Jiang'er started to patiently answer the phone. She even made calls during our interview.

I had heard she was a midwife, and though her career began in this manner, Jiang'er later became a gynecologist and obstetrician. After graduating from high school in 1970, Jiang'er was sent to a hospital to work as a nurse. As was the case of many Chinese people who started working at that time – during the "cultural revolution"

– Jiang'er learned her specialty in the field. One day, she was home when the time came for their neighbor to give birth. She and her mother went to help in the difficult, risky delivery. Jiang'er's mother left to get a doctor while the 16-year-old girl remained with the pregnant woman, who was sweating, crying, and screaming. Before the doctor could arrive, the pregnant woman had given birth to a dead baby. Jiang'er thought, 'If I were a doctor, I could have saved the baby.' Thus, the door to her destiny had just opened, and the student registered with Urumqi Institute of Medicine. Years later, she left with a diploma in her hands.

Jiang'er recounted a story about her career to me. It was in May 1980. One day when she was alone at the hospital, she heard someone calling her and she ran toward the voice, but before she could take the mother-to-be to a decent room, the woman ended up delivering the baby in the hallway. The baby's mouth was full of the mother's excrement and it was suffocating. In front of the father's horrified expression and without hesitation – and ignoring her own disgust – she practiced mouth-to-mouth resuscitation on the baby. The mother and the newborn survived.

As Chinese is not Jiang'er's native language and neither is mine, we sometimes misunderstood each other. So when I asked her how many children she has "delivered," she answered, "Only one, a girl," pointing to a young woman's photo, a graduate in computer science who works at the Urumqi Renmin Hospital. I phrased the same question differently and obtained a different answer: this time, the huge number of 6,000 babies in 36 years. The gynecologist worked at the Fuhai Renmin Hospital where six gynecologists served, until she was assigned to the Mother and Child Health Centre, which is also in Fuhai. The time is long gone when women gave birth at home, and since 2000, Fuhai is no longer on the list of the poorest counties.

On the other hand, if the workers and employees in Chinese urban areas have insurance, farmers and herdsmen remain far behind. With a system that was launched in 2003 for a trial period, the central and regional governments pay basic medical insurance for each farmer. The birth insurance covers all expenses for the workers who have subscribed, and part of the fees cover the independent rural workers. In Xinjiang, 40 counties, including Fuhai, are covered by the new system, according to Jiang'er.

The gynecologist doesn't stay in her hospital; she goes around on inspections and on education campaigns, and she teaches preventive medicine to the Kazak nomads.

Her husband, who was a driver, is now retired. Jiang'er, aged 54, still has six years to go before her retirement;

very busy at present, she has not yet planned how she will use her time. "We will see later," she added. The gynecologist says that few young people want to become doctors today. "The pressure is too strong, although the wages are reasonable," she explained. Jiang'er works eight hours a day. Doctors spend the weekend at the hospital on turn and have no annual holidays. What makes her more uncomfortable is that the centre is too small. "All the services are concentrated on 520 sq m, which is inhumane. In the sole gynecological department, we are five! We monitor women during their pregnancy and, when they are ready to deliver, we send them to the hospital. Then we follow up on the mother for one or two weeks and the child for up to six months."

From what do Kazak women suffer? "High blood pressure and anemia mostly, due to their diet. Our people are still nomads, at least partially. From May to October, herdsmen leave with the livestock and, during that period, they don't eat vegetables and fruit. We strongly advise pregnant women against adhering to the nomadic life."

From 2001 to 2004, the mortality rate of parturient mothers and newborns has been zero in Fuhai. In 2005 and 2006, there was only one death per year and that was due to the mother's heart failure. Such a remarkable record can be attributed to the improvement of maternal care and to a massive campaign for perinatal care through the management of pregnancy by updating individual files, having pre-delivery checkups, delivering in the hospital rather than at home, and conducting post-delivery visits in the home, without forgetting Jiang'er's efforts, which have been acknowledged by a series of awards. For instance, in 2006, she was one of the country's Ten Elite Women ("San Ba Hongqi Shou" in Chinese). Back in 1995, she was elected as a Model Worker – an honor rewarded by a one-week stay in the national capital. She also has an indelible memory of meeting President Hu Jintao, and it is precisely this event that she mentioned when I asked her to describe the greatest happiness in her life.

We compare traditions associated with birth for the Kazak and Italian people. "In the past, families preferred boys, but society has evolved. They even prefer not to have too many boys and have some girls, because if they have too many boys, they will not be able to marry all of them. A wedding costs too much. Providing a house for the young couple is the responsibility of the groom's family, as well as offering gifts to the bride's family members, which include grandparents, parents, uncles and aunts, cousins, brothers, and sisters."

Some of the boys that Jiang'er had helped to deliver still visit her, and some ask her to assist their wives in delivery. In Kazak language, Jiang'er is called "mother

who cuts the umbilical cord." In Italy as well, the *levatrice* is a very important person, a family member in a way. But, contrary to Italian and Han Chinese, for the Muslims, only the mother may breastfeed her baby; they have no "wet nurse."

We then took a look at the garden. Jiang'er's husband accompanied us. He showed me the apricot trees, and indicated which vine produced the best grape. Upon seeing the zucchini flowers, I asked Jiang'er how she cooked them. She had never heard that zucchini flowers were edible, so I explained how to prepare this exquisite Italian dish.

When she is not at the hospital, Jiang'er does house chores, visits relatives and friends, and watches TV, but only the news programs. She had not mentioned reading until I brought it up. As I showed interest in the stones on the windowsill, Jiang'er lit up: she collects them. Sports are not included in her interests.

During our afternoon stroll to the lake – what can I say! – to the Ulungur* "sea", she told me that she used to

---

* Fuhai is a green region. The county extends from Altay Mountains in the north to plains and desert in the south. Ulungur and Ertix Rivers flow in this fertile region and irrigate vast pasturelands. Fuhai is also the site of Alashan Nature Reserve, which is famous for its hot springs, its Butterfly Valley, and Ulungur Lake, with an area of 1,035 sq km; it is divided in two sections: the large Buluntuo Lake (or Sea) and the small Jili Lake. It is one of the 10 largest fresh water lakes in the country.

knit before but she stopped long ago. Upon smelling the roasting fish aroma, she added that she liked to cook. Suddenly, she stopped at a souvenir stand and chose a jade pendant with a red silk thread, which is the Chinese way of wearing it. "For you to remember Fuhai," she said, placing it around my neck.

Jiang'er speaks Kazak and Chinese and has not gone abroad. "Haven't you thought about visiting Kazakhstan? Don't you consider it your ancestors' country?" After a thoughtful pause, she answered: "I never thought of that. I am Chinese." She did only one trip worthy of this name. "In 2006, I was invited by the Ministry of Health to take part in a two-month trip. We visited Beijing, Shanghai, Ningxia, etc."

Discreet and generous, Jiang'er, upon hearing that I would stay in my hotel room without eating and that I would work all evening, personally delivered a "family size" bag of peaches, bananas, and plums. Readers, if you see some spots on this page, it is probably the juice from all the wonderful fruit.

URUMQI, CENTRE OF ASIA

U rumqi marks the Asian continent's centre. The exact centre is at about 30 km southwest of the city, in Baojiacaozi Village, Yongfeng Township.

The service industry represents only 1.6 percent of the city's gross domestic product (GDP); transformation and production sectors, 36 and 62 percent roughly. The

transportation industry is well-developed; the air and ground routes reach the heart of the bordering countries. Telecommunications cover the whole region and are easily accessible; my mobile telephone service and the wireless Internet connection never failed while I was there. It is common to see a herdsman among his sheep or a farmer on his tractor using a cell phone.

In Urumqi as everywhere in Xinjiang, all ethnic groups enjoy the same rights and the education level is high. Every year, 1,500 high school students are chosen to pursue their studies elsewhere in the country. The great religions, Islam in the first place, as well as Manichaeism, Shamanism, and others, coexist harmoniously.

One of Urumqi's main natural resource is the solar and wind energy, but oil and coal are not far behind. Technology, pharmacology, and biotechnology are also significant. Everywhere I went in Xinjiang – cities, prefectures, counties, townships, and villages – the sun was present. As the air is not polluted, the sun's blazing rays naturally reinforced my resemblance to the local population. I am constantly amazed to see that even the Uyghur believe that I am one of theirs, and they talk to me in their language, instead of talking Chinese to the Han who accompany me.

From the top of Hong-

shan, an altitude of 910 m, one can admire the city in its entirety and view its development and modernity. In the 1960s, 15 days were needed to go from Kashgar to Urumqi; 20 years later, six days and six nights are enough. Today, the 1,088 km between these two cities can be covered in 21 hours by train or 90 minutes by plane.

Urumqi International Grand Bazaar may be not as famous as the Kashgar Bazaar, but it is the largest in the world with its area of 40,000 sq m and built-up surface of 100,000 sq m. There, it is easy to find traditional hats of Xinjiang's different ethnic groups; furs; a large variety of scarves and foulards; chiselled silver, brass, and copper; carved wood inlaid with mother-of-pearl or metal; nuts and dry fruit; leather boots and belts; a huge assortment of little boxes made of jade, bone, lacquer, and other materials; bracelets and other jewellery; real or miniature musical instruments; natural cosmetics and medicines; stuffed camels; donkeys in company of the famous Afanti; and even more.

LOVE IS ALL HER LIFE

Dalia, Russian

Naturally, since we were passing through Altay Prefecture the girl who accompanied me would definitely want to visit her mother, who lived in the city of the same name. I had half a day to spare on my schedule; I could shorten my nights a little and find a reason not to go out for dinner, so we could spend a day in Altay.

The prefecture is all water and mountains, and four Chinese characters written in many places serve to identify it, even from the air: *Jin shan yin shui*, meaning "Golden mountains, silver waters," because long ago, the gold-diggers came here to make a fortune.

Dalia also has a Chinese name – Fang Ling – and not only for a practical reason but because her maternal grandfather was a Han. However, she identifies herself as a Russian ethnic Chinese, and so do her two daughters. In her youth, she studied Russian for six years, but as she has little occasion to use it, except with her mother on the phone, she has forgotten much of it.

Though Russian ethnics number 15,600 in China and have settled mostly in Ili Prefecture and Tacheng and Urumqi cities in Xinjiang, as well as in Heilongjiang Province and in Inner Mongolia Autonomous Region, there is no Russian autonomous prefecture in Xinjiang because the Russian don't live in a compact community. Dalia

speaks perfect Chinese, as she was born in and studied in China, in addition to Kazak, which is the official language of the Autonomous Kazak Prefecture. In fact, here, all commercial inscriptions and road signs are bilingual: Chinese and Kazak.

Dalia has been a teacher, first for five years at a middle school in Burqin, where she was born, and then, following her marriage and her settlement in Altay in 1981, at a primary school. She lives in an apartment on the campus of the largest Altay primary school, with

2,500 students and over 100 teachers. The campus is deserted now – being the end of July – and the surroundings are perfectly calm. Moreover, this calm seems characteristic of all the places I visited in Xinjiang until now, except, obviously, Urumqi.

Dalia's apartment on the fourth floor is spotlessly clean and well lit by large windows in the three bedrooms and even in the washroom and the kitchen, which is not common for Chinese houses. On the living room windowsill, three pots of fuchsia geraniums brighten up the atmosphere, behind an elegant white muslin curtain against a background of mountains. Like many Chinese women, Dalia loves plush animals and several can be found around her apartment. Santa Claus also fascinates her and this character is also a part of her decor – in many variations! This is an aspect of Dalia's Chinese taste. In fact, since the house reflects the person, I can imagine the character of the woman with whom I will spend 24 hours.

She was almost as happy to embrace me as she was to embrace her younger daughter, who works in Urumqi, when we arrived. The older one used to work in Beijing. She recently returned to Altay to complete the formalities regarding her going to Kazakhstan. There, she will study Russian for two years. Hearing the news, I was surprised and thought, 'Why doesn't she go to Russia instead?'

"Studying in Kazakhstan is less expensive," Sonia thinks it is closer, and the quality is the same. She told her mother, "Society requires skills; I am still young, it is time for me to return to school."

Dalia is only 53, but she retired in 2001; work was taking too much of a toll on her health. With two daughters who needed her, in her heart she could not bear teaching two 50-pupil classes at the same time. Her daughters became boarding students in Urumqi at the respective ages of 18 and 16; one in university, the other in high school. It is at that moment that the loving mother quit teaching and went to live in Urumqi "to cook for her," she explained, pointing to Yira, who then lived with her in a rented apartment. Dalia worried about the younger one mostly, who was timid and would easily withdraw when others would assert themselves. She worked hard to make a "sturdy woman" out of her fragile daughter. "Sonia was stronger; I didn't have to worry," she added.

She herself acquired a hardy character and even the nickname of "strong woman" through two years of the "cultural revolution" spent in a rural area. From 1974 to 1976, she worked with medical services after a six-month training period. She still spoke highly of her teacher, who was "a great doctor," she said. If she remembered that period fondly, it was because the experience had a positive influence on her. "After tasting all forms of misery, I had nothing else to fear." When her daughters were little, both lived with their mother in a le mot mud house; she had to find water at 100 m, with a shoulder pole supporting two buckets.

Dalia was very happy with her teaching job. The biggest problem was educating undisciplined children who were not compliant and whose parents were very demanding. Dalia is capable of much love, and "love is what the young people need," she claimed. "I had a physically disabled student whom I chose as a class leader. You can't imagine her gratitude," she recalled. When Dalia's name was mentioned in her presence, the girl would smile radiantly: she knew she was loved. "Here, boys are still preferred to girls. At home, girls must serve their brothers and give them their all. I try to make the parents understand that the same importance and the same attention should be given to both sexes, and when they understand that, the girls are happy. I also have been loved less than my brothers."

Pushed by her mother, Yira chose English as her major. She was a good student who, like Dalia, always liked to learn. In the presence of my company during this documentation tour, she never missed a chance to ask how to say this or that in Uyghur, Mongolian, Kazak, and most of all, she remembered, while I didn't. In her

last year of high school, she was in a special class for
talented students. She was also excellent at ping-pong,
swimming, skiing, and skating. She liked to dance and
sing, play the accordion and guitar, and has studied
drawing. She said: "As you return to Beijing, I will start

to paint again." She also wishes to master the Russian language, and for the time being studies it on her own.

After she retired, Dalia became a tutor in the Chinese language for Kazak students. Their school requires a minimum number of students to hold a Kazak language class; if the minimum number is not filled, children have to attend the Chinese class and may have problems following mathematics, as the teacher speaks too quickly for them. Uyghur students, on the other hand, were numerous, and presently have their own school.

How happy the teacher was to hear recently that two of her three students had attained the grade of 80 this year! The third, who got 60, continued his lessons during the summer holidays but at a relaxed pace. Dalia charges 200 yuan a month from each child, while her colleagues ask for 230 or 250. "I tell the parents, if their child studies well and progresses, I am satisfied."

As soon as Dalia returns home, she listens to the radio and plays a CD. "I love to listen to music." She keeps herself in good shape with long sessions of bicycle riding every morning, skipping rope, and skating in the winter. "She swims like a fish," Yira added.

That day, she prepared *baozi* stuffed with eggplant, carrot, *piaz* (onion) and mutton meat. Excellent! I filled up and asked for more at dinner. The next day, she arose early, and, without making a sound, prepared all kinds

of pastries as well as pancakes, which she served with a variety of homemade jams: peach, strawberry, apricot, and even blueberry, a fruit that I had not seen anywhere else in China. There were also fresh butter and clover-scented honey.

Dalia is also a good cook. She knows her nutrition and the nutrient value of each vegetable, fruit, meat, and fish. In May, she was invited on a CCTV-2 program for a cooking demonstration. For her, everything that can be eaten is prefaced with a "did you know that?" such as "Did you know that eggplant, especially the peel, can awaken the auto-immune healing power; that this fruit activates blood circulation and this other one delays the aging process?" This is the kind of book Dalia enjoys reading, and she has become the guardian of a treasure trove of knowledge.

At 18:00, when the blazing sun died down, we strolled in Hualin Gongyuan, the Birch Forest. Following Xinjiang time – two hours behind Beijing – it was still light at 22:00. In the little Altay city, all 200,000 habitants seemed to know each other, which made taking a walk very pleasant.

Among this woman's accomplishments, what she does even better is to love her fellow humans. Her personality displays generosity, empathy, understanding, and a genuine desire to help. From her I keep, besides a deep impression of her character, a bracelet in "desert jade" with a Pixiu, a Chinese mythical creature who feeds itself with gold and silver and thus protects one's fortune.

GONE WITH THE SOUND OF A FLUTE

Eerdexi, Tuva

S ince I was near Kanas, I expressed my intention to see a man I had interviewed two years earlier. Eerdexi (pronounce Erdesh) lived in the far north of Xinjiang, two steps from the Sino-Russian border. Tuva people have their own spoken language but no written system. Tuva is a rare language that belongs to the Turkic group*. But I was told that Eerdexi had died last spring. However, I can't help reporting his words from that time because Eerdexi was then a "living fossil" of Xinjiang Tuva culture.

As with most names in the locality, Kanas is a

---

* The Altaic family has about 60 languages spoken by 250 million persons, divided in three groups, this is the **Turkic** including Turkish (50 million), Turkmen, Uyghur, Kazak, Uzbek, Kirgiz, Tuva; the **Mongol** including Khalkha or Mongol as such, Ewenki; and the **Toungouze**, including Manchu, Oroqen, etc.

Mongolian word and means "fertile and mysterious place." The Tuva number about 180,000 and are mostly established in Baihaba Village, Hemu Tuva Village in Burqin County, and Kanas Village.

Eerdexi was 68 when I met him in 2005. "We all descend from Genghis Khan and his soldiers," he said, "and we have been living here for generations." According to some researchers, they might be descendants of weak and ill soldiers left behind by the Great Khan, while in the case of some old Tuva, the ancestors could have migrated out of the Siberia Tuva Republic 500 years ago.

In the past, Tuva people lived on hunting. "We are

no longer nomadic," specified Eerdexi, adding that nowadays, the Tuva are mostly farmers and shepherds.

"When I was a child, we needed three to four days to get to town by horseback or by a cart pulled by a horse. Now, we have good roads." However, they are not practicable the whole year long. In the 1950s, there could be up to two metres of snow. Today, there is less snow, but transportation is not yet smooth. Temperatures may dip as low as -40°C sometimes. But the Tuva don't remain prisoners in their village in the winter.

"Look at these skis," indicated Taiban, Eerdexi's

niece, who served as an interpreter. "The bottom is covered with horse hide. The hair allows smooth passage on the snow while they serve as brakes when one traverses a hill."

A bow on the wall, almost two metres long, was still used in games and festivals. Its string was made of leather. Eerdexi's modest house was like a museum with a variety of relics of Mongolian culture, especially Tuva, such as a wooden milk bucket, and wolf, marmot, and fox skin.

As the Tuva practice Buddhism, each home has a little altar dedicated to Buddha. One can also see the 10th Panchen-Lama's photos on the altar.

Excitedly, I awaited the opening of "the box" containing Eerdexi's most precious possession. "We Mongols have four special musical instruments, including the well-known horse-head violin. The fragile instrument in this box is a *shu'er*. Sixty centimetres long, it is made from a cane called *halate cao* that can be found only here, at Kanas, and harvested in September. Its stalk is naturally empty." I took the instrument to examine it. It was extremely light, like an egg shell. "You see the three holes," Eerdexi continued, "we pierce them for the fingers to cover them naturally, without any contortion."

Other materials have been experimented with in the making of the flute, but the perfect sound can only come from the *halate cao*.

"I am the last one to play this instrument. After me, it will no longer be heard. I will play one of my compositions for you – *Wonderful Kanas*." He played a very delicate tune, which was airy, languorous, and melancholy. I had the impression of hearing two instruments at the same time: one being a fixed tone and the other one, the melody. I remarked on this to the flutist. "Right," he answered. "It depends on the placement of the tongue and teeth on the instrument. The fixed sound is produced by the blowing, the melody by the fingers."

Why are there no persons who will carry on this tradition? "Young people today," said the artist, "are not patient. They learn for one or two years, then let it go. This instrument, as simple as it looks, is very difficult to play. I started at the age of nine, and only at 22 did I perform in public. The younger one starts, the better it is."

But Eerdexi didn't condemn contemporary youth. "The young have other talents. They can speak several languages, such as Tuva, Mongolian, and Kazak, because of the environment, and Chinese, as the national tongue; even English for those who study." Local children start school at seven. Before, there was only the Mongolian language school; today, they also learn Chinese. For high school, they go to Altay. Then they pursue higher education at Inner Mongolia Normal University or Xin-jiang Normal University. Some attend Minzu (Nationalities) University in Beijing.

Eerdexi's house was built by the family about 40 years ago. It was all made of Siberian red pine, including the furniture, in contrast with the nomadic Mongols who live in yurts (tents). The family income was due to tourism for a large part. They rented rooms to travellers and horses for riding.

It has not been that long since the Tuva began getting

married to others outside the clan, with other branches of Mongols but not other ethnic groups. The Chinese family planning law allows the Xinjiang minorities to have three children. If all three are the same sex, couples can try for a fourth. Eerdexi – it was long before! – had three boys and four girls and three of them had married. One of the boys was a teacher, another studied *shu'er*, and the last one was a herdsman. Two daughters were married, the third was a singer, and the youngest still attended school.

Eerdexi played two more compositions. Around a low table, we sat comfortably on carpets, savoring the homemade cookies and pastries, milk candies, dry cheese, yogurt, and butter tea. Taiban brought a pitcher of *nai jiu* (milk alcohol). The singer-daughter came in, looking elegant in her Mongolian dress with a decorated headgear. She sang, with a *hada* on her arms and a glass in one hand. When she offered the alcohol to me, I dipped my ring finger in it, and flung one drop towards the sky to honor the gods, one drop to the Earth who feeds us, and one to the inhabitants of the house, before drinking it. Then, she passed the *hada* around my neck as a sign of respect.

Eerdexi has left us. His soul has gone away with the sound of the flute but his souvenir remains among us. *Aqita!* (thank you), refined musician!

TO GUIDE THE MUSLIMS

Abdurakip·Damullah Hadjim, Uyghur

"The role of an imam is to set an example for Muslims. If he doesn't, it is useless to be an imam." This is one of the first sentences uttered by Abdurakip during our two-hour talk, as soon as I returned to Urumqi from north Xinjiang. He had been very busy in recent days, having returned the day before from Turpan where he was born and raised. Just before meeting me he had met with a Shanghai delegation that wanted to know more about Islam in Xinjiang. Despite the rushed situation, he didn't show any impatience or fatigue and answered all my questions with the smile of a man who speaks of what he loves and what motivates him.

Abdurakip is his Uyghur name. Damullah indicates that he is an imam of the highest level, and Hadjim

(superior to Hadji) shows that he has accomplished the ritual pilgrimage, or *hadj*, to Mecca.

Born into a rural family, he attended a Chinese language school. At the end of high school in 1979, he didn't pass the university admission exam. His disappointed mother wanted to make a useful man of her son and introduced him to imams. The young man began studying Islam under their guidance. "When Deng Xiaoping, the engineer and initiator of the China's reform and opening up, declared that religious belief is a human right and a personal choice, and that religious practice must be protected by the Chinese Constitution," stated

Abdurakip, "I decided to throw myself into the study of Islamic texts and to become an imam," adding, "We no longer live in the time of the 'cultural revolution,' when religion belonged to the old ideas that China had to get rid of." Today, most religions are present in Xinjiang.

Abdurakip speaks perfect Chinese and Uyghur, and good Arabic, as he studied in Egypt. Most Muslims, according to him, know enough Arabic to make it the language in which they pray. From 1980 to 1990, he was instructed by imams in several cities. Between 1991 and 2001, he himself was an imam in Turpan's Shanshan County at the Id Kha Mosque. One can also see the synonymous terms Idkah, Idgar, or Atigar, which mean "a place to celebrate festive days."

How does the day of an imam unfold? His role consists in guiding his Muslim brothers and in leading them in the practice of their faith. This starts with the five daily prayers: *Bamdat, Piexin, Digar, Sham,* and *Hoptan*, which are recited, respectively, half an hour before sunrise, at 13:00, at 17:00, at sunset (a different time every day), and, finally, some time after *Sham* that last until dawn the next morning. Each session lasts half an hour and is preceded by ritual ablutions. "The imam absolutely must go to the mosque to pray. If he prays alone at home, he doesn't set an example for anyone," said Abdurakip. Also, he must wear the appropriate turban and robe.

The other Muslims – the common faithful – take part in the prayer whenever possible or they delegate a family member to replace them. At each prayer session, between three and 100 persons attend the mosque. The others pray at home or in their hearts.

Friday is a sacred day, *al-jumu'a*, a word from Syriac language meaning "day of reunion". Thousands of believers go to the mosque at 12:30 to listen to a 30-minute teaching in the local language, which is Uyghur or Kazak, or Chinese for the Hui. It is the imam's function to explain the scriptures and to remind them of

rules such as respecting women, assisting parents, and so on. Half an hour of prayer in Arabic follows this. Those who don't know the language comport themselves quietly and listen. Advanced students or imams-in-training lead the ceremony, while senior imams stand behind to observe and correct them. Regardless of the weather – wind, snow, rain, or heat – the mosque is full, as well as the outside square. "This accommodates 10,000 people, and this is not an exaggerated number."

The rest of the time, the imam attends to his personal work: the farmer cultivates his land, the merchant looks after his business, and so on. As for Abdurakip·Damullah Hadjim, he functions as the director of the Xinjiang Islamic Studies Institute and is also a professor. He teaches 10 hours a week. The 170 students are all male.

How does one become a Muslim? "By conversion, such as for a Han who wants to marry a Muslim woman, or by birth to a Muslim family," the imam explained. "There is no special ceremony at birth. The child is trained to practice little by little, but he has no obligation before the age of 18. But afterwards, if he fails to fulfill his duty, he will be punished." I then asked which sanction awaits the young man, and the imam answered, "Such a man will never reach happiness; he will have a miserable life."

I didn't want to contradict my interlocutor, who

seemed convinced that all his Muslim brothers are faithful practitioners, but, according to Prof. Feng Jinyuan, an expert in Islam from the Institute of World Religions under the Chinese Academy of Social Sciences, only 50,000 to 100,000 of the 20 million Chinese Muslims strictly observe under any circumstances the commands of their religion, including *salat* (prayer) five times a day, facing Mecca.

When someone dies, the imam conducts the funeral and the situation is instructive. Muslims bury their dead three metres underground and the site itself is covered by an empty tomb above ground.

In a wedding the imam also has a role to play; when a man and woman know each other well, are in love, and want to start a family together, the imam is called upon to marry them. The ceremony takes place at the bride's home. After prayers, advice to the young couple, and exchanges of marital commitment, a piece of *nang* (bread) is dipped into a bowl of salted water, and the spouses eat it. The newlyweds don't wear a ring or other visible symbol of their union. The couple receives a marriage certificate from the People's Republic of China as citizens of this country and an Islamic certificate befitting Muslims. Celebrating a Muslim marriage is a function of the imam, while taking part in the following banquet is a personal choice.

I have noticed that Uyghurs often drink alcohol, and I asked Abdurakip what he thought about that. "Alcohol is strictly forbidden to Muslims. It is not right to drink alcohol, but as anywhere in the world, there is good and bad," he said. On the contrary, for example, if women don't go to the mosque, it is a habit in Xinjiang, not a prohibition. Normally, women can enter a mosque, but they have to cover their arms. However, they cannot enter during menstruation. Foreign tourists can enter but they must respect the rules.

Ten Muslim ethnic groups lived in Xinjiang 1,000

years ago. In China – the country where among the highest number of ethnic groups and religions coexist. Isn't that amazing? Unfortunately, in some parts of the West, Islam is not so well-known and people ascribe agendas to Islam that have nothing to do with its foundations but that belong to groups of extremists that China, along with the rest of the world, fights fiercely.

Upon reflection, this is a miracle of harmony. Before Islam was introduced in China, Zoroasterism, Buddhism, Taoism, Manichaeism, and Nestorianism were already being practiced in Xinjiang, due to the Silk Road, and propagated at the same time as primitive local religions and Shamanism. After the introduction of Islam, not only was the coexistence of several religions maintained in Xinjiang but Protestantism and Catholicism were added.

Abdurakip is 45 years old and his wife is 10 years younger. The couple has three daughters of 14, 9, and 6. When I went to their home to take a picture of the girls and their mother, the youngest was asleep and the mother was not home. The older two were very polite despite their shyness. I commented to the second one, "You paint your eyebrows?" and her father answered with an affectionate smile that she was already a lady. In fact, Uyghur women often draw a black line joining both arches of their eyebrows. It surprised me when I saw that on my first visit to Xinjiang but I became used to it. A

nation's criteria of beauty are not universal.

The imam has been to Mecca three times, heading a delegation of Chinese Muslims in 1994, 2000, and 2005. Before the foundation of the New China in 1949, only 42 Chinese Muslims had been to Saudi Arabia. Starting in 1980, with the restitution of religious freedom, there have been at least 3,000 a year; their numbers increase year after year and has now caught up with other countries' averages, and 30 percent are women. Every year, 12 to 15 Xinjiang persons, one per prefecture and municipality, are chosen and their pilgrimage expenses are covered by the state. The others go independently or are subsidized by Muslim institutions. I often hear people joke, "When they are young, they have no money to go, and when then have money, they are too old." I asked what the criteria are for selecting the lucky few who will benefit from a free trip. "Their level of Islam knowledge. This means that before 50, one is seldom ready because of work, the children to educate.... After 70, it is too late because if anything were to happen abroad, such as a heart attack or a respiratory failure, who would be responsible?"

Abdurakip is from a non-educated, peasant family. How did he reach such a high level at his young age? He answered, "I had a goal, and I walked straight toward it, working very hard." The Institute of which he is in charge is one of 10 of its kind in the country; 58 persons work there.

The imam told me about a 23-day trip he made in Syria, by way of the Netherlands and Italy. Once, he went to Cairo via Thailand. Cooperation with Egypt in matters of Islamic education is very strong and, presently, 64 Muslims from China study in that country. Being curious, Abdurakip asked me about life in Italy, a country about which he wanted to know more. In 1994, he went to Saudi Arabia, and, in 2000, to the United Arab Emirates, always in the capacity as an imam. He frequently goes to Beijing, the national capital, for meetings and congressional functions mostly. In his free time, he adores reading, especially books on religion. His remaining leisure time is occupied with sleep.

RETURN TO THE EAST

Lindai, Mongolian

"Return to the East" is both a period of Mongol history in China and the title of a huge painting by Lindai. When Lindai was a child, his father told him the story of their Xinjiang ancestors who were dispersed in the 18th century. Readers, it is necessary that I summarize here the saga that up to this day influences the life and the work of the man I will introduce to you.

The Mongols are one of the 13 most ancient ethnic groups established in Xinjiang. They arrived after Genghis Khan in the 13th century in an expedition north of the Tianshan Mountains. During the Ming Dynasty, the Mongols were divided into two groups: the Tartars in the east and the Oryats in the north of the desert. In the mid-16th century, the Oryat people were divided

again into tribes: Turgut, Dorbüd, Huxut, and Junggar.

In 1630, to avoid the threat of the increasingly powerful Junggar, the Turgut tribe commander led his people and army in what is today the Volga Basin. But Tsarist Russia rapidly turned their lives into a living nightmare. Not only were the Turgut made to pledge allegiance to the tsar, Russia had interfered in their internal affairs.

In 1761, Wobaxi became the Turguts' commander. A great number of them had been forced to fight for Russia and sacrifice their lives in the battles. The distressed Turgut people yearned for the day when they could be liberated from the tsarist yoke. Wobaxi took advice from other commanders and decided to accomplish his people's dream: return to the East. At the end of 1770, Wobaxi diverted Russia's attention and gathered his people for the great departure. On January 1, 1771, he launched his elite forces in a surprise assault against the enemy garrison. Then, heading 33,000 families, or 170,000 persons (according to various sources, the numbers ranged from 50,000, 80,000, and 100,000), he headed east, crossing the frozen Urals and then the snow-covered Kazakhstan grasslands, despite the Russian cavalry that dogged them. Eight months later, after a succession of ordeals and losses, the Turgut contingent finally reached motherland Ili, north of Xinjiang. The Qing government (a Manchu Dynasty close to the Mongols) sent representatives to welcome them and to help them become established. A group continued south to Hejing County in Bayangol (Bayingolin) Autonomous Mongol Prefecture, an area equivalent to one-third of Xinjiang. To pay homage to the hero Wobaxi, the Emperor invited him to his summer residence in Chengde and conferred upon him the title of "khan." Wobaxi died from illness in 1775 at the age of 33. Wobaxi's remarkable exploits shook and excited the world at the same time. The Turgut people have contributed enormously to the development and prosperity of multiethnic China.

Lindai painted several independent pictures related to this historical period, but his major work is a 6.35 m × 2.1 m panorama, which include 200 characters: the elderly and children walking painfully in the snow; men and women bearing luggage on their shoulders and dying from cold and hunger; people on foot or horse or camel, dragging cows or goats; people carrying the sick and wounded on their backs; and all trudging along with individual expressions of misery – the whole reflecting the ordeals encountered on their journey.

In 2002, to celebrate the third anniversary of Macao's return to the motherland and the 230th anniversary of the Turgut people's return to Xinjiang, Lindai was invited to exhibit this work in Macao. It is now kept at the local museum of Hejing County.

"Return to the East" ("Dong Gui" in Chinese) is becoming Hejing's "trademark," as well as a commercial trademark, I noticed.

Lindai, born in Hejing in 1966, belongs to the Turgut group. With a portfolio of about 400 paintings, he is one of the youngest Mongolian artists and one of the more representative of the Mongol style. Seventh of eight children of a herdsmen family, he used to look after sheep from the ages of six to 14. Predisposed to art even then, when he was on the pastureland, he drew on the earth or snow and made little clay animals. Only at 14 did he

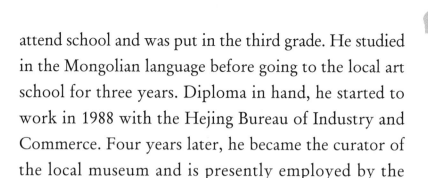

attend school and was put in the third grade. He studied in the Mongolian language before going to the local art school for three years. Diploma in hand, he started to work in 1988 with the Hejing Bureau of Industry and Commerce. Four years later, he became the curator of the local museum and is presently employed by the Hejing Bureau of Culture and Sport.

Lindai and his wife Jinghua, a bank employee, have two daughters, 16 and 11. The eldest, Xiurong, had only one week of summer holidays before her last year of high school, which is decisive for her admission into university. As of this writing, she favored the sciences. The little one, Surguk, was more attracted by the arts:

singing, dancing, reciting poems, drawing, and painting under her beloved father's aegis. Both girls studied in a bilingual school (Mongolian and Chinese) and have learned English from grade one. By contrast, their father learned Chinese by himself and speaks with a very strong accent. Their mother also attended a unilingual school. When she started to work, she registered for a Chinese course and on her own learned enough of the Kazak and Uyghur languages to perform her job. "Oral Uyghur has only 24 consonants and eight vowels, and 27 modified

Arabic letters and five Persian in the written; Mongolian, 32 letters; and Kazak, 15 vowels and 25 consonants. These languages are easy to learn!" Jinghua encouraged me. Lindai teaches art to students ranging in age from 10 to 36. In 2007, the family bought a 140 sq m first floor apartment in a new building. Each girl had her own bedroom, the living room was immense, and another room held oil paintings, calligraphies, and ink drawings. I noticed a black and white photo of Lindai's father framed with a ribbon of mourning; the man had died only two months earlier. On the table, an oil portrait of his father had just been completed.

The artist had his workshop in the basement and I walked through as though entering a sacred place. Lindai unrolled the charcoal sketches for me of his "Return to the East" on which he had been working for 14 years. "The greatest difficulty is in the clothing. No illustrated documents exist, so I must use my brain to imagine them in conformity with historical reality." In 1995, Lindai, his father, and his uncle went to the Republic of Kalmukia where they collected clues for three months. "There are some documents but no costumes." Back in China, Lindai worked one more year to achieve his panorama. Among the trips that Lindai had made, that one impressed him deeply. He also visited Inner Mongolia, Chengde City, Kazakhstan, Qinghai Province, and Russia, all places that could possibly reveal secrets relevant to his research.

Another immense painting, 17 m × 2.3 m, covered a whole wall, its left and right extremities rolled up. The artist had been working on it for two years and needed at least another year to complete it. Its theme, as ever: Return to the East. Lindai complained that he lacked time. Every day after coming home from the office, he paints for four hours. "The costume problem remains the most difficult to solve. And, I must imagine the lives of these peoples during their eight months of trekking, all of their daily acts. Over here, you see, is a love story while they travelled," he indicated to me.

In his free time, Lindai likes to paint and cook. The day I visited, he asked a colleague to help out because his wife and his older daughter were coming back only for lunch, and he had reserved his time for my interview. We had boiled mutton meat with potatoes and carrots, a dish that the Mongols call "meat to be eaten with the hands." The shoulder blade meat must be eaten totally. Lindai used one of the two big knives on the table to divide, separate, and free the meat from the bone for each guest to have a piece. Exquisite! It is really the most tender part.

Unfortunately, I missed being able to take part in a joyous family gathering, when the Mongols all meet on the grassland, set up a tent, sing and dance, play games,

such as lassoing a horse or riding a skittish horse or even a billy goat, and roast a skewered mutton. When they tear the meat apart, they hang a leg in a joist of the tent – higher than their heads – for good luck. This is what I saw in the video Lindai showed to me, as I could not see the real thing and, as I watched and took notes, the artist was busily drawing me in his sketchbook.

It happens that Lindai designs sculptures such as the tall white statue of his father and his elder uncle that can be seen on the grassland, 200 km from Hejing. It represents the "returnees" to the motherland. Lindai also fills painting orders for businesses or private collectors.

Mongols practice mainly Tibetan Buddhism or Lamaism, but Lindai's family is not religious. This seems to be the case of most Hejing's Mongols, as the great

وقۇ ـ اعارتۇ سوتسياليستىك وسزاماندا ئندىرۇ قۇربلىسى
ۇشىن ، حالىق ۇشىن قىزمەت ەتۇي ؛ وندىرىستىك دەگبەك جانە
قوعامدىق امالياتپەن ۇشتاستىرلىپ ، مۇرال ، اقىل ـ وي ، دەنە ،
ەستەتيكا جاقتا رناق جان ـ جاقتىلى جاتتلگەن سوتسياليزم ستەرىسك
قۇرۇشتشلارى مەن ٴزباسارلارىن جەتىلدىرۇي قاجەت

Kazak language

194

Baluntai Temple (*Huang Miao*) is 60 km from the city.

The five hours I spent in Lindai's company gave me a chance to "soften" him. Being extremely serious at the beginning of the interview, he grew relaxed and smiling by the end. He is not very talkative, but his youngest daughter Surguk, on the other hand, would make an excellent TV anchor. And this is what she aims to be. Why not?

MY FRIENDS, THE WOLVES

Gendengjiap, Mongolian

It was by chance that I met Gendengjiap, 38, a Mongol from Hejing County in Bayangol Mongol Autonomous Prefecture who had been one of Lindai's students. Gendengjiap explained that he didn't paint anymore. After 13 years of this trade, he started a little business besides practicing charity. He makes items from goat, yak, and Tibetan antelope horns. Don't worry, he doesn't kill the animals but collects carcasses that people find in the mountains and take to him.

He also has wolves, which was what first attracted me to Gendengjiap's shop. While strolling on the pedestrian street that opened in Hejing two years ago, I saw three superb beasts made of synthetic material and covered with real wolf skin. Two of them still had their teeth. The eyes? One would believe that they are the

original owners'. I have always admired this social, intelligent animal, which is so badly known and maligned because of ignorance and prejudice. In defence of the wolf, I wrote a children's story – not off limits to adults! – where a mother wolf asks a goat for help and these traditional enemies thus finally become friends. Published by the Canadian Hurtubise publishing house, *Chèvres et Loups* was later converted into a 24-minute animation by China Central Television. I also have recently translated Jiang Rong's *The Wolf Totem* into French. I absolutely wanted to own something of the wolf to feel

closer to it, for instance, a wolf fang that was in the shop. I made my choice at the counter, and, at the end, Gendengjiap generously offered it to me.

In the shop I could see goat skulls, a yak head, and several ornamental "paintings" composed from horn pieces of different colors. One of them won a national award. They sell for about 800 yuan (80 euros or 100 dollars), and tourists like them but the pictures are difficult to transport. Gendengjiap knows that, since he is the local Tourism Office director. Every evening, after office hours, he works until midnight, planning the workers' jobs for the following day.

Presently, Gendengjiap has six employees, all young men, who have been with him for six months to three years. The youngest is 16. They are all high school graduates who could not find work and they learn the trade at a pace according to their aptitudes. Some need six months; others, one year. They work eight hours a day from 10:00 to 13:30 and from 17:00 to 21:00 or 22:00. This is a normal timetable in Xinjiang, where the summer is very hot and where there is a two-hour gap with Beijing time.

Gendengjiap invested a great deal in this enterprise. He gives his employees not only their salaries but accommodation, meals, and social security. All profits are rolled over into his business.

The little shop produces goods in four categories. First, articles with a Return-to-the-East theme, a historical event that rightly belongs to the Hejing Mongol community to exploit. Second, things related to the Mongol nomadic and rural life, such as kitchenware or

equine gear. Third, articles belonging to the Junggar Mongol tribe, though Gendengjiap is Turgut, that aim to perpetuate and proliferate Mongol history. And, finally, local souvenirs, which sell the best because of their small size and weight, such as woven bags, antelope-

horn rings, incense burners, and *hadas* (silk scarves) from Tibet.

Hejing is very pleasant, though not a destination place, but, rather, a place where one passes through to go somewhere else. The reason is that its tourism attractions are not that convenient to reach. The closest, according to the Tourism Office's director, is the Baluntai Temple of the Tibetan Buddhism's Yellow sect, 60 km away, and the most distant is the vast prairie that everyone talks about in Xinjiang but that few have seen, and Swan Lake, both 300 km away.

Also, the tourism high season is short and only lasts from July to September, explained Gendengjiap. In winter, the temperature is -20°C on the plain and -40°C in the mountains, and all is covered with snow. Few foreigners visit Hejing, but in June this year, 20 tourists came from the United States. In 2008, the road to the mountain will be passable and tourism will surely benefit from this. Already, some holiday villages (*Dujiacun*) and about 30 rural families welcome tourists. Visitors can stay in these households, which have all been accredited, and participate in daily rural life. They can ride horses or even yaks, and the animals are kept in reins. Song and dance performances are performed with visitors in mind. When I asked how many days on average the tourists stay in the *Mujiale* (herdsman's family) and *Nongjiale*

202

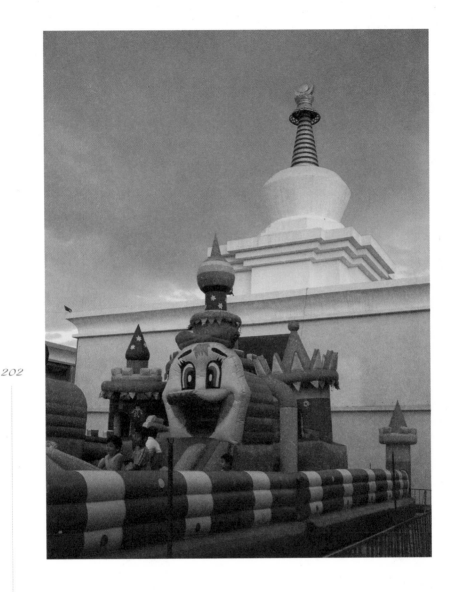

(farmer's family), Gendengjiap answered, "No, not days, only hours.... They have lunch and leave." He added, "Our principle – and I often repeat it to the authorized peasant households – is, 'The tourists arrive here happy; they must leave happier'."

I FOUND MY CITY

Ever since I arrived in Xinjiang, I've teased friends and relatives by saying that I would move here. In fact, it was not a concrete decision but an expression of just how much I liked this place. My friends and family think that, since I live in Beijing, I already am too far away – and it takes an additional three hours to land in Xinjiang!

In Xinjiang, I could use my cell phone and access the Internet wirelessly everywhere, which allowed me to keep in contact with the rest of the world and to meet deadlines. Though in 16 years I have not finished (and who could?) exploring the Han culture in the Chinese capital and travelling extensively around the country, I am so fascinated by the many aspects of the colorful Xinjiang culture and history that I did not have to be talked into establishing here and focusing my research on this wonderful region. That is why, during my investigation in producing the book you now hold, I "searched" for my possible pied à terre, appraising the qualities of each place. For the duration of my visit, every city, county, or village pleased me.

For several days I was in Bayangol Mongol

Autonomous Prefecture, in Korla, a city known in Australia, Canada, and the United States for its delicious pears. I tasted what I thought were the pick of the crops at the beginning of the season but I was told that I was eating last year's harvest; the 2007 pears would be ready in two or three months.

Korla is a young city, built a little over 50 years

ago, and is very modern, open, and pleasant. It has been called a "charming city of China" by the United Nations Educational, Scientific, and Cultural Organization (UNESCO), a title that is well-deserved. It's hard to imagine that Korla was created from practically nothing –

from the vast Taklimakan Desert. South of the Tianshan Ranges, it belonged to Nanjiang or South Xinjiang. It is in fact an oasis in the desert, created on the foundations of a very ancient kingdom.

Korla is a Uyghur word, meaning "to see very far," to the horizon as well as into the future. That is exactly the impression I had upon landing: my gaze stretched to the infinite, and I could sense the never-ending vastness.

Korla, with a population of 438,000, has 23 ethnic groups, including Han, Hui, and Mongol, the three most numerous. Its landscape varies from the snow-capped mountains to the sandy desert and from the huge lakes to the large grasslands and prairies.

What made me like Korla even more was hearing that it has a winter without snow that lasts only three months, and that a leather jacket or a wool pullover is enough to keep a person warm. If its summer is mild, I would never complain about the weather!

Bisected by the Peacock River (Kongquehe), the city exudes fresh vitality. The river welcomes swimmers of all ages and, where swimming is not allowed, Chinese and Mongolian signs make the boundaries clear. The river banks, recently converted into a large promenade, provide lovers with a romantic atmosphere and offer solo walkers a chance to contemplate significant artworks. Different by day and night, the Korla ambiance is always extraordinary. Living by the water is a possible dream, and at a reasonable price. The street system was planned with the rising number of cars in mind and is free of traffic jams.

No swimming

Korla industry and trade are progressing rapidly and at a healthy pace. There, all the products from other big cities in the world can be found. Remarkably clean, Korla is renowned for its environmental protection practices. Moreover – and what is especially worth noting – its inhabitants are particularly welcoming.

IN THE REALM OF THE TARIM DEER

Liu Hexin, Hui

Xinjiang is a vast land for breeding animals: horses, cows, sheep, and even deer. Before introducing Liu Hexin, I must speak of the Xinjiang Production & Construction Corps, which have played and will always play a major role in the development of the region. The Corps was founded in 1954 to ensure the food supply of the army and to support the local agricultural production. They were first composed of soldiers, but, during the "cultural revolution" in the 1960s, middle and high school students, of whom some were from Shanghai, joined the contingent. In the beginning, the Corps took care only of the cereal and edible oil supply. Little by little they entered all sectors: agriculture, industry, and scientific research.

This "army" had been entrusted by the state with

producing arable land and protecting Xinjiang, which is a border region of China. The Corps has been the main force of Xinjiang economic progress. One-seventh of the autonomous region's population, they have created one-fifth of the agricultural output and provided half of the export goods. When, 50 years ago, the "soldiers" arrived with their families, wasteland and desert were everywhere. They faced extremely difficult conditions and lived in tents or "*diwozi*," a type of cave dug under the ground and covered with a straw roof above ground level. Piggybacking the material and tools, they constructed reservoirs, dug canals, levelled fields, planted forest belts, built houses and roads, and established high-quality farms and even cities, including Shihezi, Kuitun, and Ta heng. Visiting these cities today, one can hardly imagine that these were desert mere decades ago.

The miracle was renewed before my eyes. Going south from the oasis-city of Korla, I saw the abrupt transition of greenery to the large expanses of sandy terrain, with, occasionally, cotton, corn fields, or abandoned spaces where wild herbs, spiny bushes, or red willow grew. From the car, I could see squares of planted straw that contained the sand. Once rooted, the straw is cut down at 30 cm. On the 160 km we drove, the wildest of nature alternated with these bits of man-made arable land, which were clutched from the desert!

Still in Bayangol Mongol Autonomous Prefecture, I suddenly saw a sign: Team No. 31, then No. 32, and finally No. 33, where I had an appointment with Liu Hexin. The production brigades have kept these designations until now.

Liu Hexin is in his mid-30s. His parents, also born in Xinjiang, were members of the Xinjiang Production & Construction Corps. Liu still lives where he was born. After graduating from Shihezi Institute of Agronomy, he refused several offers to return to work with Team No. 33, on the territory of Yuli but with an independent administration. The teams are part of a superior division

called "Shi," and the Bayangol Shi No. 2 is endowed with raising Tarim deer (in Chinese "Tahe malu"). When Liu Hexin started to work, they had to lay the foundation by preparing the soil for cultivating clover, fresh or dry according to the season, to feed the deer two or three times a day, and Liu has not forgotten how many mosquitoes there were then! From the first day, the young man used techniques that he had studied. He observed the animals' lives, as well as their growth. Breeding began in the 1970s and already there were 1,000.

What is the purpose of raising deer? It is not to eat the meat or to save the species from extinction. This ani-

mal is not endangered; it belongs to the second category of animals under state protection. The Tarim deer is raised exclusively for the medical use of its antlers. But don't jump to conclusions: no deer is killed. In the wild, males lose their antlers once year; if they don't fall off naturally, the deer get rid of them by butting a tree or ground very hard.

Before entering the farm, staff as well as visitors must spend 10 minutes in a sterilizing cabin, because the deer are very sensitive to some microbes.

"A deer cost 20,000 yuan in the beginning," said Liu, "then the price went down. It is rising again because the domestic market is not significant and because countries, such as New Zealand, having the largest herds, can influence the market. South Korea itself buys more raw material than Canada, Russia, New Zealand, and China combined."

The farm totals 14,000 heads, and Team No. 33 has 1,300. Deer are grouped according to age and sex. In one group are the eight- and nine-year-olds; in another, the four to six. Males are grouped together, and the females, with their fawns. The female gives birth once a year after a 250-day pregnancy. Usually it has only one fawn but sometimes it gives birth to two or even three at one time.

"In the beginning," Liu continued, "the farmers around here raised deer using traditional methods. We have taught them scientific methods, and we continue to follow up and give them advice, in agriculture as well. In 1999, we started to use artificial insemination but without good results since we lacked knowledge. With time, research, and experience, in 2002 we achieved good results compared with the northeast, where they obtained 100 percent in the three-week rutting season, while we reached 70 percent in one week."

The year 2003 is significant in Liu's career because he took part in the National Seminary of Agronomists on Artificial Insemination in Beijing, and he came back not only with more knowledge but with an award presented to him on this occasion: the prize for remarkable accomplishment in artificial insemination.

"A fawn born in June has 15 cm antlers in December," explained Liu Hexin. "In May and August of the following year, we can cut its antlers again. A two-year-old male grows one set a year and those between three and 10 years of age, two a year." Certain deer species, such as the Northeast or Altay, have very long antlers but few branches. Tarim deer have a flourishing set, which raises profitability. And, Liu explained, "Antlers have three parts; the upper third is of first quality. It is what we export to Republic of Korea and Japan. The top three cm sell for 50,000 yuan a kilo. Middle and lower parts are used domestically." The Shi No. 2 farm doesn't

alter the product. "We tried in 2002 but discontinued it." Reaching 100 percent profitability remains one of Liu's goals.

People easily believe in the virtue of deer antlers. Isn't that part of its mythology? Liu is convinced of the *lu rong* (Chinese equivalent for "antlers") beneficial effects because he tested it on himself, as did several of his peers on themselves. *Bencao Gangmu (Compendium of Materia Medica)*, written by the famous Li Shizhen (1518-1593), mentioned its beneficial deeds, such as purifying the blood, reducing fatigue, and so on. Liu said that those who ingest deer antlers don't catch colds, and, for them, three or four hours of sleep are as good as an eight-hour night for others. Deer antlers exist in powder, capsules, or dry slices to be infused in tea or soup. After taking the natural medicine for 20 days, one can feel its beneficial effects. As with several other traditional Chinese medicines, deer antlers don't halt illness but strengthen and preserve health.

Knowing that a deer can live 20 years, I was surprised not to see 15- and 20-year-old animals at the farm. "From the age of 12 or 13 years, a deer is no longer productive," answered Liu. "Before, we used to send some of them back to the wilderness. Now, we keep them until they die of natural causes, or we sell some to farmers, but at a loss. Deer meat is good meat, but very few Chinese eat it. We don't have the right to kill the deer ourselves; it is a state regulation."

The deer seem to be timid animals but more curious than timid. After looking over visitors, they slowly edge closer and let people caress their muzzles. Liu feels tender toward them. Each one has its own personality. During the mating season of September to November, the males become violent; they fight, often becoming wounded, and one has to be very careful around them. Mating partners are scientifically matched according to the individual health file; a male has his own stable of 13 to 15 females. In the summer, animals remain in the shadows in a corner of the pen; in the winter, there is little snow and the deer adapt to a weather of -20°C.

In front of Liu's office is a round building, a community centre for meetings, cultural activities, and recreation. Liu Hexin said he doesn't feel lonely in this place which is populated with only people who raise deer. "The teams alternate in organizing performances. We have television and I play chess with my wife," asserted Liu with conviction. Books must be ordered and food is almost all local. Both Liu and his wife enjoy cooking, and they tend a large kitchen garden. Liu likes to take walks and, a long time ago, he used to play guitar, but today he prefers to listen to *guzheng* music on disc. Their daughter studies painting.

As each team has 20,000 to 30,000 persons – not all military, since many are civilian farmers – the number of children justifies the existence of a kindergarten, a primary, and a middle school. Furthermore, students

must go to Korla to continue school. "We must think about the well-being of the growing generation and provide our children with a good educational environment," added Liu Hexin. His 11-year-old daughter is now in a boarding school as her parents are very busy. During her absence, a cat with its kitten occupy her bedroom. Liu is presently responsible for Teams No. 32 and 33, including work supervision, long-term planning, fund raising, and epidemic control. It turns out that he can't go home at night, so he sleeps in his office. Sometimes he lunches at a friend's place or at the cafeteria. Twenty-five workers are on the farm, all of them men

"because the work requires physical strength."

"In the 10 years I have been here, there have been remarkable improvements: better living conditions, new houses, paved streets, environment planning." Each worker has his own house and Liu's has two bedrooms, a living room, and a washroom without a toilet. The kitchen is outside, and the "w.c." is under the trees.... In a region so scarce in water, a bucket under the sink substitutes for a pipe, and its contents are used to water the garden.

Liu became a member of the Communist Party in 1998. "This is very important to me. The Party inculcates in us strong morals and the spirit of serving our fellow creatures." I encouraged Liu to tell the story I read about him, but his great modesty obliged me to recount the story myself, while he confirmed, "Yes, that is correct." A woman originally from Henan Province, a mother of four, was completely deprived of her means when her husband lost the use of his legs. Liu lifted her out of her misery by supplying the family needs with his own savings. She vows eternal gratitude to him. "It was my duty," he concluded simply.

Before leaving Liu Hexin, I can't help but ask him his views on desertification, a problem proportional to the size of the Xinjiang autonomous region. While going there, I noticed that several sections of Tarim River had dried up. Finding this situation hard to accept, Liu remains optimistic. He instead drew my attention to all the greenery in this area, immediately northeast of Taklimakan Desert. Everywhere were productive fields and rows of poplars. All this had been produced by the labor of the Xinjiang Production & Construction Corps. All this arable land had been captured from the desert's mouth! However, the sand pursues its rapid advance at a firm pace. Is this because Xinjiang is too large for its population? Is it because whatever land is not needed, vast expanses are consequently abandoned? According to Liu, the major reason is the lack of water in south Xinjiang. "All that is planted can grow in the desert, if there is water. No water means death for certain," he said with a dejected expression.

Liu Hexin, who had been at my disposal for seven hours, even thanked me. "It was my duty and an honor to inform you."

AS IN THE PHOTOS

When I was a child, I had a dream: to see Egypt's great pyramids. I have not seen them yet. Since I've been living in China, I have had another dream: seeing Taklimakan Desert. My dream became a reality. As I was very close to the third desert of the world, I asked the local authority representatives who were accompanying me to Liu Hexin's place for an interview, if there was a place where I could contemplate the "absolute desert" – where I would see only sand without vegetation. It took them only a moment to organize this. Half an hour later by car, I started to see dunes at the horizon; they looked like mountains. When the car couldn't go any further, we continued on foot to my great delight.

At first, we walked through spaced herbs one metre

high; we continued among brambles that hooked onto my skirt. Then I saw a trickle of water, like a tiny stream trying to forge a path for itself. One of the men placed a tree trunk over it and a block of hard sand so that I could cross easily.

We arrived at the dunes, and I took several photos, thinking it was a once-in-a-lifetime opportunity. I thanked my companions for bringing me not to the border of the desert but into it. Surprised, Liu Hexin asked, "You don't want to climb a dune?" Amazed and happy, I immediately removed my shoes.

There were three dunes – from near to far. I climbed the first one quickly, barefoot in the hot sand. The wind assaulted my ankles with stinging grains of sand and the sensation was that of a cold water jet. On top of the first dune, while taking a photo of its perfectly cut crest, I saw the wind blurring the top of the furthest dune. We hurried as a storm was coming. The little grains of sand on my legs were like needles now.

I climbed the second dune more quickly. A few metres from the top, the wind threw me down onto the soil. Someone was immortalizing this moment in a photo and I was already half-covered with sand, asking myself whether I would be able to find my shoes. The wind became so ferocious that we couldn't continue climbing. The "queen" of the dunes was only a shapeless cloud of sand that seemed to shout to me: "Away, intruder!" It was impossible to photograph the cruelty that chased me, as my camera, full of sand, had stopped working.

Climbing down was easy enough as my heels dug deeply into the sand. It was like being on escalator that was going twice the normal speed. My shoes were waiting quietly for me. I didn't even have to empty them of sand. At the bottom of the slope, it was perfectly calm.

I could not believe my eyes: not only had I "seen" the Taklimakan, but I had entered it. However, I also felt as though I had violated a sacred place, a sin not

without consequences, as I was deprived for the rest of my trip, not only of my camera but also of my voice recorder. *Mea culpa*! Hadn't Tusipbek told me, when I interviewed him: "Rain and sand are the worst enemies of a photographer. When they start, one must immediately put the camera away."

Oh! Great Taklimakan, whose name means "Whoever enters does not exit alive," you didn't take my life, but will you forgive me my intrusion?

MY KIRKIZ FAMILY

This morning I got off at Artux ("Atushi" in Chinese) train station. Artux is the administrative centre of Kizilsu Kirkiz Autonomous Prefecture. It took 12 hours from Korla in a comfortable and modern two-level train. The Artux population is composed of 300,000 Uyghurs, 130,000 Kirkiz, and 30,000 Han. After a warm welcome and a Uyghur-style breakfast, I was on my way to Ulugqat ("Wuqia" in Chinese) County. The distance is 100 km. The landscape is astonishing; the mountains are all different in shape, color, and relief that I had admired from the train – peaks, curves, indented – and continued to fascinate me along the road. What can I say about the road that is paved and smooth and lined on both sides with two or three rows of poplars in a place where few vehicles circulate! "All the greenery you see here has been planted by man," said Ms. Xie, who took charge of me at the station. "Before, this was desert." This is easy to believe when one sees mountains totally of rock or arid soil. What remains of the old streams is only a trace; even the rivers have dried up. "This year is a drought year," said some defeatedly, while others specified that "as soon as it rains, it floods."

But how to lay out such a huge territory, canalize the waters, construct reservoirs, and build dams with such a limited population, while at the same time take care of the welfare, education, medical care, economic development, and so many other headaches?

When we left Artux, the altimeter indicated 850. At Wuqia, we were at 2,150 m above sea level. At 2,000 m, we saw 20 or so wild camels with flat humps. On this vast, uninhabited land surge one can see the occasional small mud house or sun-dried brick house and with electrical wires running along the way. Once more I saw that the Constitution article that stipulates that "all the citizens of China have equal rights" is not full of empty words.

Kirkiz people are one of the 13 most ancient nations of Xinjiang. I had seen the Kirkiz in folk shows, heard their music on disks, and appreciated cultural reports about them on TV, and then I finally saw them in person. Not only that but I had actually shaken hands with several

of them, especially Toktonur, of Wuqia Information Office, Aikumar, a journalist, and Mammetjiuma, a television program director. The spontaneous hand-shaking between men and women, young and old, and natives and strangers at first perplexed me. I was then told that it is obligatory for the Kirkiz. For the Tajik, two men instead kiss each other's hand, while two women kiss on the mouth, and a woman kisses a man's hand.

The Kirkiz language, as well as the Uyghur language, belongs to the Turkic group. I found it very harmonious with all these "r" resulting in a mellifluous purr. In Xinjiang, the Kirkiz use a modified Arabic alphabet and write from right to left, while in Kirghizstan, they use the Slavic alphabet and write from left to right.

Unable to live for two or three days with nomadic rural families (because of threatening floods in that season) as I passionately had hoped, I instead visited Yektelik Village. In 1985, an earthquake – they are frequent in the Kirkiz Prefecture which is at the 40th parallel – cost 23 lives. Wuqia County has only 53,000 habitants, 80 percent of them Kirkiz. Yektelik Village, where 267 households or 967 persons live, has a kindergarten, a primary school, and a middle school. As stated before, each Xinjiang village has a health centre where both a doctor and a nurse work.

I was first invited to enter the house of a local retired

official, Hare, a father of four. Only Gulimaina, 17, was home. She has two older brothers and one married sister, who has two children. There is a gap of 20 years between Gulimaina and her elder brother. At the end of the summer holidays, the student will attend Ili Teachers College. After graduation, she will return to the region "where there is a terrible lack of teachers," she said enthusiastically.

She introduced me to the colorful needlework decorating the four walls of the large living room – her mother's work – as well as the bedding in perfect order on the huge *kang*. I asked why there were 16 blankets and a huge pile of pillows. Her father answered, "We Kirkiz don't send our friends and relatives to the hotel when they pay us a visit. It is our duty to offer hospitality."

As the winter is cold and the snowfall heavy, even the family horse wears a woollen "suit." The bag on its back is made of two large pockets that hang on both sides of its flanks. Each family has at least one horse, because "if not, how can you move out?" remarked the young girl.

Doors, furniture, timbered ceilings, and beams are adorned with floral patterns and hand-painted arabesques, and the comfortable sofas are covered with carpets and cushions. We had just entered when *nang* (bread), torn in pieces, and bowls of freshly made yogurt were brought

to the tables. There was also "milk skin" as they call the dried milk surface cream that one takes with a piece of *nang*. The two youngest boys wore their national costume for me, and the father put on his felt hat and the camel wool coat that was hanging from a beam.

Taking leave of our hosts, we went to a middle-class household, the one of Maimaijiang ("Maimai" is a variation of "Mahommed," as well as "Mammet"). There, the walls were whitewashed, without any embroidery or carpet in the living room; the floor was covered simply with a light green felt, which reminded me of conference table covers long ago, and the house was extremely clean. The hospitality was the same as in a wealthy home: *nang*, cream, and yogurt. However, the couple and their one-

year-old baby disappeared suddenly. I waited for them to return before tasting the yogurt and complimenting them. Were they busy? Were they shy? I learned that visitors are left alone so that they can eat at ease. Once "filled up," they then talk with them outside or invite them back into the living room. Maimaijiang and his wife were solemn but the mother lit up when I asked her questions about the children. The 11-year-old girl and the boy of seven were absent.

As with the whole county, this household lives on animal breeding exclusively. They have 450 sheep and 40 cows. Seven horses and two camels provide labor and transportation. Several peasants also grow chicken or practice aquiculture. What about the vegetables? The answer was that rural Kirkiz eat mostly meat. "Some also eat vegetables," added the township head, "and they buy them." However, because of the climate, Wuqia produces only apples and plums. In the summer, the evenings are cool and the winter is long and cold. What a difference compared with Artux, which is only 100 km away, where 7,000 *mu* of land were planted with vines imported from Israel that produce big, round grapes – red or yellow – called *munak yusum* in Uyghur. This kind of grape can be eaten from the end of September all through November.

I had visited two households when I was invited to

walk in the village and talk with people. On the unpaved road, groups of women and men were chatting calmly, standing or sitting on the ground on old blankets; babies were walking for their exercise; little girls were dancing; and an embroiderer was concentrating on her work. I noticed several babies in the arms of as many grandmothers who all warmly welcomed me and were happy to have their photo taken in my company. We could understand each other by gestures and mostly with the help of the township head who accompanied me, because very few Kirkiz rurals can speak Chinese. Children nowadays attend bilingual schools while their elders, who learned Chinese at a certain age, can be identified by their accents. It is honorable for the Wuqia Kirkiz to have reached 100 percent compulsory schooling of nine years. These youths will enjoy an easier life than their parents. Women over 35 are marked by their hard lives and look older than their chronological ages.

I felt at home among them. Each household has an average of three or four children. Foreigners often forget or are unaware that the rule of "one child per couple" affects only the Han, and the Han are registered as urban residents. The ethnic minorities, who make up about 10 percent of the national population and live on 60 percent of the territory, are only strongly encouraged to limit their offspring only to the number that they can

decently raise.

A 67-year-old man and his wife of 58 invited me to enter their home. In the courtyard, sheep wool – white, brown, and black – was drying under the sun. As soon as I accepted their invitation, the woman went to get fresh yogurt in a shed while her husband led me to a large room that served as living room and bedroom. The bare brick floor reminded me of old Italian houses.

The couple has raised two girls and five boys; three of them still live at home and the others are married. Peasant women consider themselves "unemployed," as they are not paid. Yet how many countless hours they spend on hard tasks! The husband, now retired, has been showing movies in the villages for 40 years. On the wall, foreign films posters outnumbered the Chinese ones.

If I can easily pass for a Uyghur or sometimes a Kazak, never have I been taken for a Kirkiz before this time. Yet, I feel a deep affinity with this people, maybe because of my longed-of dream of "living with a Kirkiz country family."

A UNIQUE BORDER GUARD

Burmakan·Moldo, Kirkiz

I would like to dedicate a chapter on the extraordinary mountains that form the major part of the Kizilsu Kirkiz Autonomous Prefecture. But such a chapter can't be written. The unspeakable magnificence of the landscape can only be experienced. Thousands of photos would not accurately reflect the fascinating rocky landforms, each one more beautiful than another, that I admired along the 500 km travelled in this prefecture, which is called "Kezhou" in short.

When I arrived in Kezhou, the legendary woman I came to interview was absent. On the eve of the 80th anniversary of the People's Liberation Army, the volunteer and unarmed "military" had been invited to Urumqi where she would be highly honored with the "national model of the people and the army" title.

Delayed the next day because she was a distinguished guest for the celebration of the PLA anniversary, Burmakan was not able to be on time for our appointment. She was impatient, thinking that I was waiting for her, but I would not miss the opportunity of meeting her and, in any case, I always have enough to occupy my time.

Burmakan had gone to Urumqi by train, a 36-hour route, of which 12 hours were due to flooding on the way. Back by plane, she landed at 15:00 and asked the driver to drive her immediately to my hotel in Wuqia, where she greeted me and embraced me like an old friend whom she hadn't seen for years.

I wanted to interview her in her environment, so

we left by car on that incredible road, which had been paved 10 years ago, crossing rocky mountains for hundreds of kilometres, to the Kirkiz village of Jigen Township, where Burmakan had spent her life. In our two-hour drive, we did not see any houses; I felt as though I had entered a dream in the core of civilization.

On our arrival, Burmakan and her husband, Toiqibiek, 80, showed us the new house that had been completed just one month before and that still smelled of fresh paint, but I chose to do the interview in the old house. Burmakan agreed happily.

Toiqibiek and his daughter-in-law kept busily slicing different kinds of melons and covering the *kang* with a variety of pastries, pouring *ma nai* or fermented horse milk with a low amount of alcohol into a large bowl for each guest. Before touching any food, one must wash his or her hands over a pewter basin while a family member pours water from a jar. Once the hands are washed, one must avoid shaking them and sponge them off with the proffered embroidered towel.

Burmakan, 65, is very lively; she likes to talk even if others don't understand her language, and she smiles constantly. She complained laughingly about the heat in Urumqi while in her village, at an altitude of 3,200 m, a light wool sweater is necessary in the evening. And there she was adding to a box of her collection of certificates

and trophies the red and golden banner she had slung across her chest from Urumqi. In recent years, as she often left her native village, she can understand a little more Chinese but doesn't speak it. Thus, Toktonur, whom I mentioned before, waited for us there. I had asked for an interpreter of the Kirkiz mother language to trans-

late to Chinese, not the reverse.

Burmakan was born to a rural family; she is the youngest of two boys and two girls. She never went to school and neither did her three sons and two daughters, who are all unilingual and illiterate. Burmakan can write her name and nothing else. But her 11 grandchildren attend or will attend school and have been bilingual since the first grade. The one-year-old grandson who played with my earrings and my pen is called a name meaning "journalist." Here is the story.

Two years ago, discovered at the frontier line of S'mukana (meaning "iron wire net" in Kirkiz) between China and Kirghizstan, were several flat stones bearing on one side the characters for *zhong guo* (China), hand-

engraved in the simplest way, and, on the other side, the word Kirghizstan in the Kirkiz language, and, on some other stones, the name Burmakan. The local authority investigated and discovered the author of these inscriptions. Burmakan had simply copied the names of the two countries from other writings. This was in 1961, when she was 19 years old. Her father used to guard the border before her. He told his children, "When you grow up, you will do as I do. Up there, there are no soldiers. It is our duty to protect our country."

This was 60 km from where they lived. It is where they led the flocks in the summer. Burmakan would spend long periods on the pastureland without returning home. At 3,800 m altitude, it is cold in August. One evening after a heavy snowfall, Burmakan could not find her way to her shelter. The snow level was half way up her leg. She was lost in the dark, so she waited until sunset to orient herself. Such misadventures were frequent and the soldiers on patrol or who were stationed in the surroundings also lost their way or were victims of rain storms or floods. Burmakan saved several of them from death. She brought them back and fed them. On our way to Jigen this afternoon, we crossed a control point at the end of the road, and the guards, seeing their "mother" in the car, let us pass without question. Burmakan is nicknamed "mother of all the soldiers."

She was so devoted to her voluntary task that she neglected her own family. One day, when it was raining heavily, she went to help a lone woman and, during her absence, her own house and all the family belongings were flooded.

From the pastureland where the tent was to the frontier, Burmakan rode 20 km twice a day, sometimes with a newborn in her arms. She gave so much of herself that her breast milk ran dry.

Another day, during a meal, she heard gunshots by the border. She left in a hurry to see what was going on. This was the final straw for her husband, who lost his temper and claimed that he wanted a divorce. He had had enough of a woman who didn't cook meals on time and didn't take care of her children properly. Eventually he calmed down and understood that she was on a sacred mission. He accepted the situation.

But what could an unarmed woman have done in the face of intruders who were attempting to penetrate Chinese territory? On horseback, she would have called on the soldiers.

It has now been more than 45 years since Burmakan has been working voluntarily to serve her country. She has never received any compensation except a pair of shoes a year. When the Communist Party publicly praised her heroism and her commitment last year, journalists

flew to her place and all the media reported her story. This is why her grandson, who was born during that wave of publicity, was named "journalist."

Burmakan's greatest desire had long been to become a member of the Communist Party. Not everyone can be admitted. Her dream came true when, last year, her achievements came to light. Her new house, to which she just received the key, is a mark of the Party's gratitude. Moreover, she now receives 100 yuan a month for her lifetime. In talking of the Party's kind deeds, Burmakan couldn't hold back her tears. "My father has not seen my new house," she lamented. "He would have been so proud. When my older sister was killed by a car that was driven by a soldier, my father told the horrified, trembling military: 'Go, go, and drive carefully. All the soldiers are my sons.' He didn't have the soldier arrested. He said it would not bring my sister back to life." And, she added, emotionally, "I went to Beijing twice, and four times to Urumqi. My poor father, never...." One of Burmakan's sons, in trying to save his mother from a potentially violent yak, was thrown from his horse and lost the use of his legs.

The "soldiers' mother" suffers from arthritis in her knees, and the altitude of nearly 4,000 m causes more problems for her. Through her example, Burmakan has planted the seed of patriotism in her whole family. She

doesn't go to the border anymore, but 10 of her family members do it in turn, including the children.

After meeting this heroic woman, we took the road back to Wuqia where we arrived around 23:00. At the hotel two representatives of the Artux Information Office were waiting for me; they had driven 100 km to say farewell. They wanted to dine with me and especially to give me a traditional headgear of the local ethnic group – a thoughtful gesture that ties me closer to "my Kirkiz family."

FROM THE IRON WIRE TO THE STEEL BLADE

Yasen, Uyghur
Upur·Rahman, Uyghur

T he tightrope walker I was going to meet, Aiskar, was out of his village for a performance tour in the country. However, Yengisar ("Yingjisha" in Chinese), 70 km from Kashgar, doesn't lack for acrobats. So I was accompanied to Yasen Dawaz place instead. *Dawaz* means "to walk on a wire" in Uyghur language. The 76-year-old man might be the tightrope walker's father, I thought, upon seeing his fit physique. I was wrong. He was the popular *Dawaz*!

From the road to his modest home made of yellow earthen blocks stacked without mortar, one must walk 600 m on a dusty path, lined on both sides with high poplars. I had never seen so many poplars except in south Xinjiang where the water is scarce and where the desert threatens to encroach further.

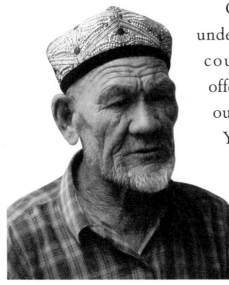

Outside the house, under the greenery in the courtyard, two *kangs* offered a pleasant space for our conversation. When Yasen's wife, 55, came back home a little later, she immediately spread out a golden silk brocade on the *kang* for the "honorable guest," me. Throughout my travels among the ethnic minorities villages, I noticed the same hospitality, the same kindness.

Yasen has three sons between 16 and 28 years old. The older two work in commerce in the autonomous region while the youngest, illiterate, lives at home. With his mother, he leaves early in the morning for the township, where both are street cleaners. The family income comes from the pair, and the family live on the few chickens and goats they raise. Yasen also had a daughter who died 15 years ago. In the daytime, the man remains at home, and he trains a six-year-old girl as an acrobat. From what I could understand, the girl is not a family member; her father's whereabouts is unknown and her mother died. Yasen was very proud of her. "She is my follower now."

But I couldn't see any exercise equipment. When I asked about it, Yasen walked into a shed in the courtyard and brought back rolls of cable, steel pegs, and the hammer that served to anchor them. How often do they work out? How strenuous is it? And what was the young tightrope walker's level of skill? I couldn't estimate it with my own eyes. According to Yasen, the youths he trained started between four and seven years old. Training starts at two metres above the ground.

Yasen began at the age of eight, following the example of his grandfather, who died at 120, if one was to believe him. I tried to have him confirm the respectable age of the late man, to which Yasen added that his father died at the age of 125. Enough of

the family legends!

If this interview is so short and contains so many uncertainties, it is because I had no interpreter; it was assumed that I spoke Uyghur.

*   *   *

At Yengisar, where the Uyghur make up more than 95 percent of the population, one can see very few cars but many carts harnessed to donkeys. This place hid a culinary specialty that I greatly appreciated: roast *baozi*. The little bags made of dough without yeast contain mutton meat and minced onions and are baked without fat. A 70-year-old widow, at the table next to mine, explained the virtues of this delicious fast food washed down with clove tea.

*   *   *

The name of Yengisar is well-known for another of its famous resources: the making of Uyghur knives. In the afternoon, I went to Upur·Rahman's shop and he showed me around. In Yengisar, there are presently seven steel-knife factories. Upur·Rahman's shop has 60 workers. It was established in 1956, and Upur·Rahman is the third generation at the head of the enterprise – since 1986. "Yengisar has been making knives for 500 years, but before, there were only little family shops," he explained. During war time, they made steel weapons such as swords and sabres. The independent workers grouped in enterprises only half a century ago.

"How is it that when I go to Uyghurs' houses, I never see the kind of knives you make here?" To my question, Upur·Rahman answered that the knives they use daily are also made in Yengisar but because they are not adorned, they cost less. Those I saw displayed in the counter are pieces of a collection that may be offered as a gift or kept as a souvenir, he added. How nice they were, sparkling in their cases, as well as the modest pocket-knives with their horn or silver handles! I could hardly make up my mind.

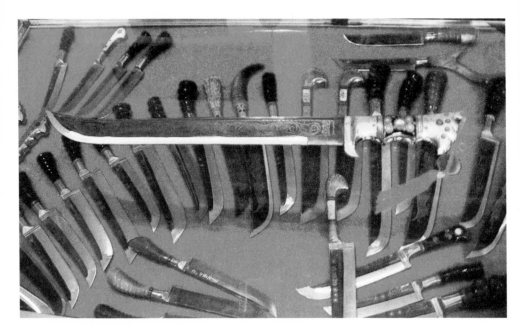

Upur·Rahman values his production at 30,000 to 50,000 units a year. His enterprise doesn't export. Whatever exporting there is, it is taken care of by private businessmen or companies.

The making of a completely hand-made knife requires 20 processes: from bringing the steel to a white heat and the striking of raw material into the shape of a knife. I saw the workers in action. The craft requires strength, meticulousness, and physically restrictive positions. However, the shop is well-ventilated, and the decoration processes are often done in the open air. Chiselled handles, engraved brand names on the blade, inlaid semi-precious stones or glass, and small shell plates – hand cut one by one – are what constitute the beauty of the knives and determine their price. After seeing the requirements of the whole process, the prices seem very reasonable to people.

*　　*　　*

The Kashgar region is rich with family shops, including those making Uyghur musical instruments such as *ravop*, my favourite. For the quality of the sound, the apricot tree, which flourishes in Xinjiang, or mulberry

wood is used. Ornamentation consists of inlaid bone or synthetic materials. The work is completely hand-made and artisans work in assembly line fashion, each one being responsible for one operation.

Elsewhere, Koziqiyabixi Village, a name meaning "pottery village on top of the mountain," has 450 households or about 6,000 persons. The buildings, which bridge over the street, are one of the local features. Cobblestones are of two kinds: if hexagonal, they indicate a way out; rectangular, a dead-end. Only one color dominates the whole: the color of both earth and wood. Beams support the earthen walls. The government has built a new area with comfortable, reasonably priced apartments, but it is not always easy to move a population that has been rooted in a place for 600 years, even if it is to better their lives. Some houses, which are still solid, have been built by several generations, each one adding a storey as needed. The potters who inherited the craft centuries ago can be counted among the local and not yet industrialized resources. Sooner or later, tourism will reach these craft villages, which are now a sleeping gold mine.

THE MIRACLE OF
AN OASIS

S hihezi rose from nothingness. Today in place of "the most suitable Chinese city to live in" (UNESCO) were wasteland and rubble a mere 60 years ago.

Visiting the city of 300,000, I saw the miracle that had been realized in the 1950s and 1960s by the People's Liberation Army, and that had soon after been reinforced by thousands of young men and women, who were mostly from Shanghai City and Shandong, Henan, Sichuan and Gansu provinces. They built cities from absolutely nothing, working with rudimentary tools that they often made, and living in more than precarious conditions. They now number 2.5 million, including the descendants born in Xinjiang, or, put another way, one-tenth of the Xinjiang Uyghur Autonomous Region population, distributed among 14 cities borne from their efforts.

At the museum, I met one of these Xinjiang pioneers, 86-year-old Du Xing, originally from Gansu. Men had come first, and, three or four years later, young female soldiers followed to establish families. Couples were matched by the authorities according

to the partners' apparent affinities and rarely by their own choice. That was Du Xing's situation, and he is still satisfied with his marriage. The museum, earlier located in the City Hall, is now in a new building since 2005, marking the 50th anniversary of the foundation of the Xinjiang Uyghur Autonomous Region.

A cultural museum has also been opened to the

Photo : Zhang Yingjun

public. Shihezi has its own university and a nationally renowned Institute of Agronomy. Huge flower-filled gardens and parks, with an artificial lake, monuments, and white pigeons, offer respite and renewal for Shihezi citizens. No barren earth is visible, as beautifully maintained grass, flower beds, trees, and bushes make this oasis on the Silk Road an enjoyable place to live.

KASHGAR, THE FASCINATING

S ome people like to talk in proverbs and sayings. I for one try to avoid them. However, there is one that I can't help but repeat: "If you have not seen Kashgar, you have not been to Xinjiang."

Kashgar shares an 888-km border with Afghanistan, Tajikistan, and Pakistan. Its famous wholesale market or International Grand Bazaar of Middle and West Asia offers dried fruits and nuts, musical instruments, wood or brass products, clothing and textiles, silk carpets, a huge variety of clothing accessories, and even a series of fashionable masks for Muslim women who prefer to cover only their faces. Merchants come from China's different ethnic groups and even from the neighboring countries. Bartering for a suitable price is part of this typical and interesting bazaar's charm. And I really doubt one will leave the market empty-handed!

Kashgar means "rich with jade." Its population is 92 percent Uyghur, and the rest are mostly Han, Tajik, and Uzbek. I was amazed at how clean this city is, even though it might be as it was during the Silk Road era. Kashgar has few cars, some motorcycles, small buses, which are rarely crowded, and carts pulled by donkeys. Most of the women wear a veil or a headscarf, and men wear a woven *doppa* or a white, knitted cap. Upon arriving from another Xinjiang city, one has the impression of awakening in a North African or Middle Eastern country. Kashgar is a must-see!

The tomb of the Fragrant Concubine, Rong Fei Iparhan, is one of Kashgar's major tourist attractions. A large building called Apak Hoja Mausoleum in honor of the famous Yusuf Hoja's son, the first to be buried there, hosts 58 (72 before a destructive earthquake) tombs of the powerful Kashgar regents' family members. Men, women, and children can be identified by the size of the tombs, and the tombs are covered with carpets or silk blankets and are personalized with the decorations.

The name "Fragrant Concubine" comes from Rong Fei's habit of bathing in water containing *shazao* (sand dates) flowers, which left a delicate fragrance on her skin. She was the younger sister of the Kashgar regent who married her to the Qing emperor as a symbol of alliance.

She lived 28 years in Beijing with Emperor Qianlong, who not only used to take her along in his inspections around the country, but learned the Uyghur language in her company.

She died from illness at the age of 55 in 1788. It is said that she didn't like the emperor and had annoyed her mother-in-law so much that the latter isolated her, which contributed to her death.

The chariot that brought back two chests, one containing the mortal remains, and the other, the concubine's personal belongings, is also exhibited in a corner of this strange cemetery, which dates back to 1640. Three years and 124 people were needed to bring back

the caskets. However, in Hebei Province, among the East Tombs of the Qing, a tomb identified as the one of Rong Fei can be seen, and, according to one interpretation, only the concubine's clothes and head ornaments had been sent back to her native Xinjiang after her death, while her remains are in Hebei.

Behind this monument is an ordinary Muslim cemetery where families go to look after the tombs or their dead every Wednesday.

The nearby mosque, all wood and brick, goes back 122 years. It is now inactive and under state protection.

Walking in the streets, I noticed a woman praying in her little store, answering the call from the minarets all over the city.

The Kashgar Id Kha Mosque is the largest in China, as well as the most influential, and its reputation has expanded all over the world. It is also the country's most representative of Muslim architecture. Every Friday, 6,000 to 7,000 believers flow to this mosque. On ordinary days, about 2,000 attend each of the five daily *salat*, and on important festive days, up to 8,000. The large mosque square, surrounded by museums, restaurants, and boutiques, is always full of life – of people walking, chatting, resting, playing, and trading. The nearby mar-

ket overflows with rare fruit, such as figs.

Kashgar is beautiful, dynamic, and charming. With abundant cultural resources, Kashgar has everything to satisfy those who truly appreciate the exotic and leaves the lucky visitor with wonderful, indelible memories.

Conclusion: The Happiness of "Belonging"

I have just finished my third visit to Xinjiang; I traveled it all over. I went to the most northern point, which is the Friendship Peak on the Sino-Russian border; the most western, on the Sino-Kirgiz border; and, in the most eastern and most southern cities, respectively Kumul (Hami) and Hotan.

Xinjiang is a region of extremes: the country's lowest depression, Ayding Lake at 154 m under sea level; the warmest place, Turpan "fireland"; the most distant point from the ocean, Tacheng; and the region bordering the greatest number of countries, eight. Xinjiang is rich with ethnic traditions, fruits, ways of cooking mutton meat, breathtaking landscapes, types of arts and crafts, and so many other rich practices that I was also deeply impressed by the rare sight of beggars, by the cleanliness of cities and villages (including the infrequency of spitting on the streets), by the moderation of voice tone and volume, and by the absolute absence of mosquitoes in big cities; what a pleasure to be able to sleep with open windows! Regarding telecommunications, QQ is much more popular than MSN in Xinjiang. On the other hand, one can't directly fund a cell phone account opened elsewhere in the country.

Xinjiang has a high number of polyglots, whose range of languages runs from Uyghur to Chinese through Kazak and Kirgiz, but foreign languages, such as English, Russian, and Japanese, are little known. A foreign visitor who can't speak the local languages will definitely need an interpreter. Posters and signs are bilingual (Chinese and the local language). Written English – where it exists – is... sometimes understandable, and mostly a source of entertainment.

I have been asked and will be again, which place and which person left the deepest impression. Trying to answer this would end in failure. Each place, from the poorest village to the most magnificent modern city, had its charm. I didn't dislike any place. On the contrary, each person I met showed human warmth and a sincere desire to help me better know his or her people or his or her place. And what can I say of the Xinjiang Uyghur Autonomous Region authorities and of their

First township west of the country – the last to see the sunset in China. (Photo: Wang Qingyun)

representatives in each locality, who took me under their wing as soon as I arrived and tried to fulfill all my wishes, to guide me, to answer all my questions, and to search for the needed information when it was not available immediately. This trip has been for me a gift from Heaven, and I can't help but thank all those who contributed to its success, all of them useful and much-needed.

How many wonders I didn't even mention, such as the stone figures of Ili grassland, the Tianchi Lake at dawn, the colorful autumn forests and the stone forests, the thousand Buddhist grottoes, the ruins of 30 or so ancient kingdoms, the Tianshan phallic rock art, the impressive Xiaohe open-air cemetery, the Kanas nature reserve, the cotton, sunflowers, and tomato fields, the snow-capped peaks, the cities sculpted by the wind, all these festivities that allow the discovery of ethnic foods, music and sports, etc. Go, Readers, seek your pleasure: see with your own eyes!

My very first impression, which was confirmed for me again and again till the end, remains in the vastness of this region, in the infinite expanse where nothing obscures the view, in the freedom that emanates from this land and its inhabitants.

Finally, I can't ignore the fact of never having heard the words *lao wai*. I have been in China long enough to know that they are not an insult, but always being called a *foreigner* digs a ditch between "them," the Chinese, and "me," the stranger, while my heart, my life, my interests,

and my enthusiasm are with these people. In Xinjiang, I encountered a totally opposite situation: the Uyghur themselves always and everywhere took me as one of them and talked to me in their language. That in itself made me smile, and, at the same time, rubbed a soothing balm on my "non-belonging" wound. At long last, I felt as though I was part of the Chinese people!

My gratitude to June Masuda for her English polishing.

图书在版编目（CIP）数据

这些新疆人：英文／（加）李莎（Carducci, L.）著.
北京：外文出版社，2008
ISBN 978-7-119-05180-2
I.这... II.李... III. 人物—访问记—新疆—英文
IV.K820.845
中国版本图书馆 CIP 数据核字（2008）第 000533 号

出版顾问　侯汉敏　　艾力提·沙力也夫

责任编辑　宫结实
装帧设计　姚　波
封面摄影　拜海提·牙合甫
印刷监制　冯　浩

这些新疆人

李莎 (Lisa Carducci) 著

*

© 外文出版社

外文出版社出版

（中国北京百万庄大街 24 号）

邮政编码 100037

外文出版社网址：http://www.flp.com.cn

外文出版社电子信箱：info@flp.com.cn

sales@flp.com.cn

外文印刷厂印刷

中国国际图书贸易总公司发行

（中国北京车公庄西路 35 号）

北京邮政信箱 399 号　邮政编码 100044

2008 年（16 开）第 1 版

2008 年第 1 版第 1 次印刷

（英）

ISBN 978-7-119-05180-2

09800（平）

17-E-3860P